TEN TRUE TALES

W9-AWY-009

WORLD WAR I HEROES

Allan Zullo

SCHOLASTIC INC.

To my dear friends Stanley and Toby Cohen,
who make life a lot more fun when they are around.

— A.Z.

ISBN 978-0-545-67533-8

12 11 10 9 8 7 6 5 4 3 2   14 15 16 17 18 19/0

Printed in the U.S.A.   40
First edition, September 2014

AUTHOR'S NOTE

Most of the soldiers who fought for our country in World War I were everyday citizens who felt duty-bound to protect and preserve the values that make America great. An untold number of them found within themselves incredible courage they didn't know they had. In the bombed-out fields near St. Mihiel, France, in dogfights in the flak-filled skies over the Somme, and in hand-to-hand combat in the Argonne Forest, Americans discovered a bravery that spurred them to reach far beyond their limits.

They became the valiant heroes of World War I.

You are about to read the gripping stories of ten of them. These accounts are based on memoirs, diaries, biographies, battle reports, and military files. Using real names, dates, and places, the stories are written as factual versions of their heroism, although certain scenes have been dramatized and some dialogue has been recreated.

Several heroes featured in this book earned the Medal of Honor — our country's highest award for valor in combat above and beyond the call of duty. Of the 4.8 million Americans who served in World War I, 119 were awarded the medal, including 33 who received it after they had died.

The ten stories spotlight soldiers, pilots, and Marines who stared the enemy — and death — in the face and still managed to carry out their missions. They were the ones who performed heroic deeds despite their fears. They were the ones who succeeded against overwhelming odds. They were the ones who helped win the war.

— Allan Zullo

CONTENTS

THE GREAT WAR

World War I — or the Great War, as it was known back then — turned into one of the largest and deadliest conflicts in all of human history.

More than 65 million military personnel fought in Europe from July 28, 1914, to November 11, 1918, resulting in the deaths of about 8.5 million combatants and 6.8 million civilians. More than 21 million combatants were wounded. Of the more than 4 million Americans who served in the war, 116,516 were killed and 204,002 were wounded.

The war was triggered by the assassination of Archduke Franz Ferdinand, heir to the throne of the empire of Austria-Hungary, and his wife, Sophie, on June 28, 1914. They were shot in Sarajevo, Yugoslavia, by Gavrilo Princip, a member of the Black Hand, a secret military organization in the country of Serbia.

A month later, Austria-Hungary retaliated by invading Serbia, which ignited already long-standing hostile relations among the major powers of Europe. As a result, the Allies — mainly France, Belgium, the British Empire (including Canada), Russia, Romania, Serbia, and eventually the United States, Japan, and Italy — waged war against the Central Powers, made up of Germany, Austria-Hungary, and later the Ottoman Empire (Turkey), and Bulgaria.

In the early days of the war, Germany invaded the neutral countries of Belgium and Luxembourg before attacking France, which led Great Britain to declare war on Germany. At the same time, Germany also struck against Russia.

At the outbreak of the war, the United States pursued a policy of avoiding any military action and instead tried to broker a peace agreement, but to no avail.

For the first three years in France, the war was fought mainly along the Western Front, which extended from the Swiss border, along the western border of Germany, and into northeastern France to the North Sea. The Eastern Front stretched through much of the Ukraine from the Black Sea to the Baltic Sea, a line nearly one thousand miles long.

Throughout the war, both sides fought from elaborate trench and dugout systems opposite each other. The fully exposed area between the opposing trench lines was called No Man's Land. When soldiers went "over the top" (leaping out of their trenches to attack), they often were mowed down by their foes long before they reached the others' trenches, which were often protected by barbed wire and other obstacles.

Because antibiotics hadn't been discovered yet and first aid was limited, relatively minor wounds often were fatal from infections and gangrene. One of the biggest killers was disease caused by poor sanitary conditions and hygiene. Many soldiers suffered from dysentery, typhus, cholera, and, in the winter, exposure from the cold and wet. Adding to their miseries, the trenches were infested with rats and also lice, which transmitted trench fever, a serious disease that caused high fever and muscle pain.

For soldiers who were on the move, they were forced to run through killing zones laced with machine gun fire and bursting with artillery. Often, the soldiers advanced far beyond their support units, causing them to go without food and water for days at a time.

As casualties mounted into the millions, all sides were employing new warfare technology, including faster-shooting machine guns, long-range artillery, poisonous mustard gas and phosgene gas, and armored tanks. For the first time in a major war, airplanes battled each other in the skies in dog-fights, carried out photographic reconnaissance missions behind enemy lines, and dropped bombs.

German submarines, known as U-boats, prowled the Atlantic, sinking five thousand merchant ships that were bringing supplies to Great Britain and France. In 1915, a

U-boat torpedoed and sank the luxury ocean liner RMS *Lusitania*, killing 1,198 passengers, including 128 Americans. Following international condemnation, Germany promised it wouldn't target passenger ships. It went back on its word two years later.

After the sinking of seven American merchant ships by U-boats and the interception of a secret German telegram promising money to Mexico if it would fight against the United States, President Woodrow Wilson asked Congress for "a war to end all wars." On April 6, 1917, Congress declared war on Germany.

Because America's military forces were relatively small in size, the federal government instituted a draft, requiring all males ages twenty-one to thirty to register for military service. (It was later expanded to males from ages eighteen to forty-five.) More than 2.8 million men were drafted and an additional 2 million volunteered for various military branches that made up the American Expeditionary Force (AEF).

In 1918, Germany launched its Spring Offensive and pushed to within seventy-five miles of Paris, the French capital. But bolstered by the firepower and manpower of the AEF, the Allies halted the enemy assault. On August 8, the Allies countered with the Hundred Days Offensive, which sent the German Army reeling in retreat. In less than two months, the Central Powers collapsed. Bulgaria and the Ottoman Empire surrendered, and the Austria-Hungary

Army gave up. Then it was Germany's turn to sign an armistice.

On the eleventh hour of the eleventh day of the eleventh month — 11 A.M. on November 11, 1918 — a cease-fire took effect, finally putting an end to the Great War.

THE TENNESSEE CRACK SHOT

Army Corporal Alvin York

Alvin York came out of the mountains of Tennessee with an education equal to that of a third grader. He had virtually no experience with the world that lay beyond his primitive life in a remote valley.

He might have been a simple man, but his mind was as sharp as his jaw-dropping talent with a hunting rifle. More keenly observant than a hungry hawk, he was quick to think and quick to react — skills finely honed from childhood encounters with rattlesnakes and bears, floods and forest fires, family emergencies and tragedies. What material things he lacked in his tough upbringing, he made up for in a wealth of common sense. He also possessed a cool head when everyone around him was losing theirs.

It was because of all those traits — along with a spine stronger than the iron he once pounded into horseshoes —

that Alvin York pulled off one of the most astounding military feats ever by a soldier during the Great War.

The third oldest of eleven children, Alvin grew up near the tiny town of Pall Mall, Tennessee, in an isolated, mountain-rimmed valley where the Wolf River branches into three forks. He lived in a one-room log cabin chinked with clay and sticks and decorated inside with newspapers and color-ful magazine covers pasted on the walls. His childhood was spent hunting and toiling on the family farm on land home-steaded by his great-great-great grandfather.

Following in the footsteps of his father, William, Alvin became an expert with a rifle and pistol and an accom-plished blacksmith. His mother, Mary, was a religious, hardworking woman, who always insisted her children do the right thing.

Like most kids in the area back then, Alvin attended a one-room schoolhouse on seats that were split logs during a term that typically lasted only two months. He eventu-ally dropped out to help feed the family by using his long rifle to hunt squirrel, raccoon, quail, wild boar, and deer. He might not have been book smart, but he learned the ways of the forest — how to stalk game; how to make medicine out of leaves, bark, and plants; how to survive in the wilderness; how to use all parts of the animals he killed. When Alvin wasn't blacksmithing or working on the farm, he hired himself out as a teenage laborer for forty cents a day.

After his father died in 1911, Alvin, then twenty-three, helped his mother raise his younger siblings because the two oldest had married. He supported the family by swinging sledgehammers and picks and axes in the construction of roads and railroads. Although he was a hard worker during the week, he was a different person on the weekends — a moonshine-drinking, rough-housing scoundrel who gambled away his wages and fought at the drop of a hat.

His mother pleaded with him to change. But for years, he refused to listen to her even though deep down in his heart, he knew what he was doing was wrong. One night, after he stumbled home drunk, his mother confronted him and asked, "Alvin, when are you going to be a man like your father and your grandfathers?"

Her words finally sunk in. He pledged he would never again drink, smoke, gamble, swear, fight, or chew tobacco. And he kept his promise. He joined her church and became known as the Singing Elder because he led the choir and taught Sunday school.

In late fall 1917, when he was twenty-nine, Alvin was drafted. At six-foot-two, one hundred seventy pounds, the muscular redhead was exactly what the U.S. Army was looking for. Before leaving for training at Fort Gordon near Atlanta, Georgia, he prayed for two days. Then he told his mother, "I received my assurance from God that it's all right that I should go, and that I'll come back without a scratch."

But neither his mother nor the pastor of their church wanted him to fight in the war because their religion forbade any form of violence. They sent a formal request to the War Department asking that Alvin be excused from serving because of religious beliefs. The papers were then mailed to him to sign, but he hesitated, telling his commanding officer, "I am a soul in doubt."

York came from a long line of patriots who fought for their country from the Revolutionary War to the Civil War. "I don't want to go and fight and kill," he told the commander. "My own experience tells me it ain't right, and the Bible is against it, too. But Uncle Sam says he wants me, and I have been brought up to believe in my country. My religion tells me not to go to war, and the memory of my ancestors tells me to get my gun and go fight. I don't know what to do. I'm a heap bothered. It's a most awful thing when the wishes of your God and your country get mixed up and go against each other."

Eventually, after deep discussions with his commander and other men of faith, York concluded, "The Bible says, 'blessed are the peacemakers,' so if a man can make peace by fightin', then I reckon he's a peacemaker." He refused to sign the papers that would have spared him going to war.

During basic training, York suffered from homesickness because he had never been more than fifty miles beyond his home.

Eventually adapting to military life, York amazed his officers with his skill as a sharpshooter, which he had

4

developed from years of practice back home when he would gallop on his horse around a tree, shooting at specific spots in the bark with uncanny accuracy.

When York was sent overseas, he was assigned to Company G, 328th Infantry Regiment, 82nd Division. Known as the All-American Division because it was composed of men from every state in the union, the unit was deployed to the Western Front in France. The Tennessee doughboy — who kept his Bible and his diary on him at all times — and his unit fought through the St. Mihiel sector and marched into the Argonne Forest. He was awed by how badly the trees were shot up and how the ground was marred by giant bomb craters.

On the night of October 5, York, who was now a corporal, wrote in his diary that "the airplanes were humming over our heads, and we were stumbling over dead horses and dead men, and the shells were bursting all around us."

Two days later, his battalion was ordered to take Hill 223 the next morning, then drive across a narrow, funnel-shaped valley surrounded on three sides by hills fortified by German machine guns. The unit's mission was to destroy the machine gun nests and fight its way to the Decauville railway, a major supply line in the German war effort.

Before daybreak, the Americans donned gas masks and moved out. Enduring a constant artillery bombardment and gas attacks, they pressed forward to take the hill. Then the battalion charged into the valley — and right into a death-trap. Firepower spewing from at least thirty machine gun nests entrenched along the commanding ridges from the front and both flanks was cutting down hundreds of Americans.

As his platoon marched forward, but not yet in range of the machine guns, York passed the wounded, many moaning and twitching on stretchers that were being lugged back to the first-aid stations. Wherever he looked, he saw dead bodies strewn among the shell craters and splintered trees. The gruesome scene of carnage reminded him of the biblical story of Armageddon.

Ahead of him, doughboys were falling left and right, like the long grass getting cut by the horse-drawn mowing machine back home. The casualties were so heavy that the superior officers ordered a halt to the advance and told the men to dig in.

The only way to continue the advance was to knock out the hidden machine gun nests on the hill opposite Hill 223. York and sixteen other men were selected for the dangerous assignment. They had to go behind enemy lines, circle around the backside of the hill, and attack the nests from the rear.

Led by Sergeant Bernard Early, the men worked their way through the thick undergrowth for about three hundred yards. They slipped past the German trenches and reached a gully behind the hill where they could hear the machine guns spraying the valley. Then they spotted two Germans with Red Cross bands on their arms. "Halt!" York shouted. Springing up like two scared rabbits, the pair bolted into the brush while the Americans chased after them.

During the pursuit through the woods, York and his comrades jumped across a small stream and unexpectedly ran into a clearing where twenty startled Germans were eating breakfast. "Put your hands up!" York ordered. Taken by surprise, the foes stood and threw their hands in the air. A German lieutenant shouted in English, "Don't shoot! We will surrender!"

The Americans discovered they had stumbled into a German battalion's field headquarters, interrupting a breakfast of beef, jam, and bread for the lieutenant, two other officers, orderlies, stretcher bearers, and runners. Except for the lieutenant, all were unarmed because they had left their weapons lying on the ground or leaning against trees.

"Keep your hands up!" York ordered. While the dough-boys pointed their rifles at their new prisoners, York trained his weapon on the lieutenant, who relayed instructions in German to the men. Wondering why the Germans gave up so easily, York thought, *I guess they think the whole American army is in their rear. Well, we ain't goin' to tell 'em anything different.*

Suddenly, one of the Germans yelled something to the machine gunners on the ridge above. As the captives dived to the ground, the gunners on top turned their weapons around toward the Americans and unleashed a lethal flurry of bullets. Firing waist-high in an effort to avoid hitting their countrymen, the gunners quickly killed six Americans and wounded another three. Early, the leader of the detachment, took three bullets in the stomach and chest.

York crouched next to the German prisoners who were still flat on the ground. Even though he was in the open, he rightly figured that the machine gunners and infantrymen on the hillside were less likely to hit him because their comrades were so close to him.

With Early down, York took command of the unit, which had now shrunk to only eight men. His fellow soldiers had taken cover in brush off to the side and out of the line of fire, but with their guns still pointed at the German captives.

As bullets tore into the undergrowth all around him, York began exchanging shots with the machine gunners. It seemed like a terrible mismatch. But the Tennessee crack shot was picking them off one at a time from a prone position just like he used to do in shooting matches back home. *This ain't no time to miss nohow,* he told himself. And he didn't. Every one of his bullets found its mark.

Whenever he saw a head pop up from the nest or any movement, he fired, killing another German. Frustrated that they couldn't hit him, the machine gunners kept yelling at him, but he didn't understand what they were saying. When there was a brief lull in the gunfire exchange, he jumped to his feet to shoot from a standing position.

While picking up a clip from a dead comrade, he spotted a German officer and five others leap out of a trench about twenty-five yards away and charge him with fixed bayonets. York pulled out his Colt .45 pistol and shot the last man first, then the fifth, the fourth, and so on until he dropped the officer last — all with one bullet each.

He wanted the rear Germans to fall first so the others would keep coming at him. That was the way he used to shoot a flock of wild turkeys back home. (As he explained in his diary, "I don't want the front ones to know that I'm gettin' the back ones, so they keep on comin' until I get 'em all.") Against the German assault, he figured that if he shot the officer first, the others in the rear would have dropped to the ground and fired a volley at him, which would have been their best chance to kill him.

The machine gunners had eased up during the bayonet charge only to watch York dispatch the six Germans, whose bodies formed a line from the trench they had come from. Returning to his rifle, he continued to shoot enemy gunners and infantrymen one by one.

If I done keep my head and don't run out of ammunition, I have 'em. He hollered at the remaining Germans on the ridge, "Give up and come on down!" They answered with more bullets. After killing a couple more — his total was reaching twenty — York shouted again, "I don't want to kill any more than I have to, so surrender!" They fired back at him. *I guess they don't understand my language or else they can't hear me with this awful racket goin' on.*

While ducking bullets, the German lieutenant, whose name was Paul Vollmer, crept over to York and said, "If you won't shoot any more, I will make them give up."

Wary of the lieutenant but willing to see if Vollmer could indeed make the gunners surrender, York pulled out his pistol and aimed it at the German's head. "If you don't make 'em stop firin', I'll take off your head — and I mean it."

Vollmer gulped and pleaded, "Don't kill me. I can get them to surrender." He then blew a whistle.

From the ridge, a handful of Germans stood up from their gun pits and from behind trees and bushes. They slowly tossed aside their firearms, unbuckled their holsters and belts, and put their hands up. Then another dozen did the same thing, followed by dozens more. In a matter of minutes, the Germans — York made a rough count of about ninety — started walking down the hill.

When they reached the bottom, he made them stop so he could make sure all were unarmed. They were — except for one who whipped out a small hand grenade and threw it at York. With lightning-fast reflexes, York got out of the way, and it exploded nearby without harming him, although it did injure several German prisoners. In retaliation, York shot him dead with the pistol.

The seven Americans who hadn't been wounded came out from the brush with their weapons sweeping back and forth at the large group of enemy soldiers.

"Let's get these Germans out of here," York told his men.

"It's impossible," said one of his comrades. "We still have to cross another enemy trench where there are more machine gun nests."

"We're goin' to get these prisoners out," York insisted.

Eavesdropping on the conversation, Vollmer asked, "How many soldiers do you have?"

He still thinks we have a mess of other soldiers with us in the woods. Refusing to reveal the truth, York replied, "I've got a-plenty." Curious, he asked Vollmer, "How come you speak such good English?"

"Before the war I worked in Chicago," the lieutenant replied.

"You should have stayed there." Seeing Vollmer drop his hands, York pointed the gun at him and snarled, "Get 'em back up. Now here's what we're goin' to do. You're goin' to line up your men in twos and do it in double time. And you're goin' to pick out some of your men to carry our wounded. I ain't leavin' good American boys lyin' out here to die. And then we're goin' to march all you prisoners back to our lines."

Vollmer carried out York's orders. The Americans were positioned on either side of the long column and told to shoot anyone who stepped out of line. Putting Vollmer at the head of the column, York stood directly behind him with the pistol pointed in the German's back. On either side of York were the two other officers. "One false move and I will kill the lieutenant and then both of you," he warned them. Poking the barrel of his gun into Vollmer's back, he ordered, "Now, hike."

Using the lieutenant as a screen, York marched the prisoners of war toward the American side. When the men reached a spot where they could either continue straight or turn and follow a gully, Vollmer suggested taking the gully.

"We ain't goin' down no gully," York growled. "That's the wrong way. We're goin' straight through the German frontline trenches and to the American lines."

As the column neared the back of the next enemy trench, the German machine gunners turned their weapons around and tried firing at the Americans. York cocked his pistol, stuck it at the base of Vollmer's neck, and said, "Blow your whistle, or I'll take off your head and" — referring to the other two officers — "theirs, too."

The lieutenant blew his whistle, signaling to the forty or so additional gunners to surrender. All except one did as they were told. At York's insistence, Vollmer twice ordered the lone German to give up, but the gunner remained at his post, his weapon still aimed at the column. Reluctantly, York shot him. "I hated to do it," he told Vollmer. "He was probably a brave soldier boy. But I can't afford to take no chances, so I let him have it."

After clearing the German front line and neutralizing the threat of flanking machine gun fire, York now was faced with a new challenge — getting his prisoners and comrades safely to the American side. On the way back, they were constantly under heavy shell fire, so he had everyone double-time through the danger zone. *There's nothin' to be gained by havin' any more of 'em wounded or killed,* he thought. *They done surrendered to me, and it's up to me to look after 'em.*

With so many prisoners, he also knew there was a danger that the Americans' own artillery might mistake the column for a German counterattack and open up on the group. But

York marched his prisoners without further harm to the battalion command post, passing gawking doughboys who cheered him. Lieutenant Joseph Woods, Assistant Division Inspector, could hardly believe it. After counting the prisoners, Woods said, "York, have you just captured the whole German Army?"

"No, sir," York replied. "Just a tolerable few — only one hundred thirty-two."

After turning over the prisoners, York and his men eventually rejoined their outfits a few hours later. Fighting their way to the Decauville railway, the Americans cut the Germans off from their supplies and forced them to retreat.

The next day, regiment officers visited the spot where York had taken his prisoners. They counted the bodies of twenty-five Germans that he had killed and found thirty-five machine gun nests that he had silenced.

The six dead Americans were buried on the hillside where they lay. Marking their graves were wooden crosses capped by the helmets the soldiers had worn.

In his diary, York wrote, "I am a witness to the fact that God did help me out of that hard battle; for the bushes were shot up all around me, and I never got a scratch."

York was immediately promoted to sergeant. An official battle report by division headquarters said that York's heroics "had a far-reaching effect in relieving the enemy pressure against American forces in the heart of the Argonne Forest."

A few months later, following a thorough investigation, York was awarded the Medal of Honor by General John

"Black Jack" Pershing, the commanding general of the American Expeditionary Force. France awarded York the prestigious Croix de Guerre for his feat. When asked to describe York's feat, Marshal Ferdinand Foch, head of the French military, declared, "it was the greatest thing accomplished by any private soldier of all the armies of Europe."

York didn't see it that way, writing in his diary that he and his comrades "had done the job we set out to do."

On May 22, 1919 — six months after the armistice was signed — York returned on a troopship to the United States. Arriving in New York, he was given a ticker tape parade, carried on the shoulders of members of the New York Stock Exchange, and honored with a formal banquet. He was then taken to Washington, D.C., where members of the House of Representatives gave him a standing ovation.

In June, a week after he was discharged from the service, York married his sweetheart, Gracie Williams, in an outdoor ceremony in Pall Mall attended by several thousand admiring fellow Tennesseans.

York refused to profit from his fame and turned down tens of thousands of dollars in offers to make appearances, endorse products, and sell rights to his life story. "I didn't go to war to make a heap," he wrote in his diary. "I went over there to help make peace." The war had changed him; he was no longer the simple mountain man. "I knew I wasn't like I used to be. The big outside world I had been in and the things I had fought through had touched me up inside a powerful lot. . . . I was sort of restless and full of dreams and wanted to be doing something and I didn't understand [what]. So I sat out on the hillside trying to puzzle it out. Before the war I felt the mountains isolated us and kept us together as a God-fearing, God-loving people. They did that, too, but they did more than that. They kept out many of the good and worth-while things like good roads, schools, libraries, up-to-date homes, and modern farming methods."

York lent his name to various charitable and civic causes. Throughout the 1920s, he went on speaking tours to raise money for his Alvin C. York Foundation, which focused on improving schools in rural Tennessee because he considered an education the key to success. He later said he was disappointed that only one of his eight children went on to college, but he was proud that they all earned high school diplomas.

Because he spent so much time on charitable work, York ended up in serious financial difficulty, so he sold the rights to his story to a movie producer. The film, called Sergeant York, was released in 1941. Gary Cooper, the star who portrayed York, won the Academy Award for Best Actor in 1942. The money York earned from the film helped him get out of debt.

During World War II, York attended war bond rallies and raised funds for war-related charities, including the Red Cross. Following a stroke in 1954, York suffered from poor health and spent parts of the last years of his life in a wheel-chair. He died at the Veterans Hospital in Nashville in 1964 at the age of seventy-six and was buried with full military honors in the Pall Mall cemetery.

THE FLYING FOX

Royal Flying Corps Major William "Billy" Bishop

His heart beating faster than the pistons in the engine of his biplane, fighter pilot William "Billy" Bishop spotted three unidentified aircraft heading toward him and his small squad of planes. As the trio flew closer, there was no doubt they were Germans; the painted black iron crosses on the wings were now clearly visible.

The young Canadian, who was flying for the British Royal Flying Corps (RFC), didn't care that the average life-span of a pilot on the Western Front was a shockingly brief two weeks or that he had been there for only a week. He was too keyed up because he was about to engage in his first aerial dogfight.

When the German planes approached the squad to within four hundred yards, the Brits turned their planes to face the enemy. One of the foes dived, then came up again and began to shoot at the last plane in the squad. Reacting quickly, Bishop swooped down and then around, flying straight at the attacking plane from the enemy pilot's blind side. Bishop opened fire and watched his tracer bullets rip into the German plane. Seconds later, it rolled over on its back and went into a spinning nosedive.

Although he was a rookie aviator, Bishop knew the Germans often faked being badly hit to trick their attackers into quitting the assault. As much as he wanted to believe he had scored his first victory, Bishop needed further confirmation, so he flew down after the plane. Sure enough, after descending a thousand feet, the German pilot pulled out of his dive and leveled off.

Gripped with an overwhelming desire to destroy this aircraft, Bishop banked his plane until he was forty yards behind his adversary, and opened fire again. He shouted with joy when he saw his smoking bullets striking the fuselage within inches of the cockpit. For the second time, the German went into a steep dive and spurted away from Bishop.

Suspecting another ruse and totally oblivious to what might be happening to his companions in their battle with the other German planes, Bishop chased after his foe. Although his plane was capable of doing one hundred twenty miles per hour on a level flight path, Bishop was diving at speeds approaching two hundred miles per hour.

Nevertheless, the German seemed to be heading down even faster. But this time the pilot didn't pull out of his dive.

He crashed nose first and at full speed into the pasture of a farm near the French town of St. Leger.

Leveling out at fifteen hundred feet, Bishop gazed down at the crumpled ruins of the enemy plane and allowed himself a brief moment to exult in his first shoot down, or victory, as it was called in World War I.

After the first flush of pride and satisfaction faded, Bishop was seized by an uncomfortable feeling. He didn't have the slightest idea where he was, because he had lost all sense of direction on this overcast day. Nothing else had mattered to him except shooting down the plane with the big black crosses. Now he began to fear that he was alone over German-occupied territory, which meant he needed to get out of there in a hurry.

But there was a problem — a big one. During his long dive, lubricating oil had filled his engine, causing it to stop. The young pilot tried everything to get it started, but the engine wouldn't even sputter. He had no choice but to glide to a hard landing, not knowing if he would end up in hostile or friendly territory.

Deciding to go with his gut, he turned the plane in the direction he hoped was toward his aerodrome and coasted lower and lower. Gliding over a French village, he saw that it was in ruins, many of its peasant homes still smoldering. His heart sank. *I must be behind enemy lines,* he thought. *My flying career had just begun, and now it will end.* He fretted that he would suffer the worst fate imaginable for a pilot of the Royal Flying Corps — becoming a prisoner of war after landing in German-occupied territory. Those unsettling thoughts were only enhanced by the sound of machine gun fire aimed at him from the ground. *I'm definitely behind enemy lines.*

Angling away from hostile fire, he continued to coast helplessly toward the ground. *It can't possibly get any worse.* Still, he wasn't ready to give up just yet. Seeing a patch of relatively smooth pasture among the rough terrain, he made one last turn and glided to a safe — for the moment — landing.

Bishop wasn't armed, so he grabbed the only thing he could use for a weapon — a simple flare gun, which offered just a small sense of protection. He jumped out of the plane and ran to a nearby bomb crater to hide while he figured out his next move.

While waiting for his fate to play out, he saw four soldiers creeping toward him. *Oh, no! Germans!*

Born and raised in a middle-class family in the small town of Owen Sound, Ontario, Canada, the blond, blue-eyed Billy Bishop dreamed of being a pilot ever since he was fifteen years old. Days after reading newspaper accounts of the first heavier-than-air flight in Canada by fellow countryman John McCurdy in 1909, Billy tried building his own aircraft. He constructed a crude version of a glider from wood, cardboard, wire, and string and then lugged it to the top of his family's Victorian home. After he got onboard, his glider slid off the steep roof and dropped straight down, crashing in a heap on the lawn below. He crawled out of the wreck slightly injured but with his dream of flying still intact.

Billy refused to apply himself in school and instead put his energies in his favorite activities — hunting, horseback riding, and swimming. He turned into an expert marksman and an accomplished horseman.

He was attending the Royal Military College when war broke out, so he joined the cavalry as an officer in a Toronto militia regiment called the Mississauga Horse. He and his comrades crossed the Atlantic in a difficult fifteen-day voyage in an old cattle boat with seven hundred seasick horses. Training in England, he became disillusioned about his impending role in the war. As much as he loved horses, he considered cavalry camp a smelly, disgusting place far removed from the battlefield where he wanted to be.

One July morning in 1915, after days of nonstop rain, Bishop was slogging knee-deep in mud and manure while checking on a line of horses. Unexpectedly, an RFC biplane landed in a nearby field. The pilot asked directions and then took off. As the aircraft disappeared into the distance, Bishop thought, *There's only one place to be — up above the clouds. I'm going into battle that way. I'm going to meet the enemy in the air.*

He took a step closer to his goal by transferring to the RFC. Although he wasn't able to get into flight school, he was sent to the next best thing — a school that would train him to be an observer, an important role in the war. Flying with a pilot over enemy-occupied territory, the observer watched where artillery shells landed and, using Morse code, directed the big guns for better accuracy; took photographs so British mapmakers could trace each detail of the German trench positions; conducted reconnaissance missions of troop movements; directed rescues of downed aircraft; and sometimes dropped handheld bombs. Sure, he was disappointed that he couldn't be a pilot, but at least he was in the air and not in the muddy trenches.

Bishop carried out his observation duties in a plane that sometimes flew fifty miles inside enemy territory — often through anti-aircraft fire. Although he kept a machine gun with him, he never got to shoot it at a German plane. However, when his plane flew low along the German trenches, he enjoyed letting loose with a burst of machine gun fire as a morning greeting or a good-night salute.

After suffering a badly injured knee during a crash landing, Bishop went on sick leave for six months. When he returned to active duty, he was thrilled to learn he had been accepted into flight school in England. Later, having earned his wings, he was shipped back to the Western Front in March 1917. The twenty-three-year-old Canadian joined No. 60 Squadron, which was based on a farm near Arras, France, and considered Britain's top fighter group. Pilots flew the Nieuport Scout, a single-seat biplane with a narrow lower wing and a machine gun mounted on the upper wing.

In his first few sorties, flying as high as fifteen thousand feet, he could see for miles around. The rolling, sprawling farmland had turned into water-filled, shell-pitted battlefields. Pastures were scarred by hand-dug trenches and tank tracks. Most days he saw rising plumes of white smoke, each one marking a French village that the Germans had sacked and torched. Seeing the senseless destruction enraged Bishop, and he yearned for the chance to attack an enemy plane.

He was fully aware of the frighteningly short average life expectancy of a new pilot in that sector. German aces were shooting down five British aircraft for every German plane lost at the hands of the less-experienced Brits. Because of the great need for pilots, the RFC was sending newly trained ones like Bishop to the Western Front with only a few hours of flying experience.

On one patrol during his first week, he got separated from his squad, became lost, and was nearly shot down by anti-aircraft fire. Because he could barely control his aircraft and had trouble with his landings, Bishop seemed as if he wasn't cut out to be an aviator. On March 24, he crash-landed during a practice flight, which was bad enough. Even worse, he did it in front of General John Higgins, who was so angry he ordered the young pilot to return to England for further training. But before Bishop was shipped out, No. 60 Squadron's new commander, Major Alan Scott, convinced Higgins to let him stay until a replacement arrived.

It was the very next day that Bishop claimed his first victory when he shot down the faster and better-armed German fighter plane, the Albatros D.III. And it was then that Bishop was forced to land because of engine failure and feared he was about to be captured by four approaching soldiers. To his great relief, the troops were British. They told him that he had just barely crossed over into friendly territory — by only 150 yards. Bishop and the soldiers then moved the plane out of the sight of the enemy where it was later dismantled and trucked back to the aerodrome.

General Higgins personally congratulated Bishop and rescinded the order for the pilot to return to flight school. A few days later, Bishop was named a patrol leader. He was leading a six-plane sortie over enemy territory when they were ambushed by ten Albatros D.IIIs that burst out of nearby clouds. Flaming bullets flew past his left wing. Discovering that a German was right on his tail, Bishop thought, *He has a dead shot on me. There's only one way I can get out of this.* With full throttle, he pointed the nose of his aircraft straight up and did a backward loop as the enemy flashed past underneath.

Fifteen minutes into the intense dogfight, the Brits had lost two planes. Now outnumbered ten to four, Bishop and his comrades hid in the clouds to evade the enemy flyers. But a fifty-mile-an-hour gale had driven the Brits farther behind German lines. Bishop led his squad back, but it wasn't easy. Flying straight into the teeth of the wind, they made little forward progress and were easy marks for anti-aircraft fire, so they had to dart from one cloud to another for protection.

The next day, Bishop recorded his second victory, so Major Scott allowed him to fly "lone wolf" missions — solo flights into enemy territory — in his free time.

On one such flight on April 7, 1917, Bishop planned to attack one of the many giant German observation balloons that floated from eight hundred to three thousand feet high behind enemy lines. They were tethered to the ground by strong cables attached to special winches that could swiftly pull them in. Observers in the baskets of these huge, elongated gas-filled balloons — which the Brits derisively called "sausages" — used powerful telescopes to spy far into the Allies' lines. The balloons were protected from air attacks by anti-aircraft guns and swarming German fighter planes.

Five miles into enemy territory, Bishop circled a balloon and began firing at it. Just then, he heard machine guns directly behind him and saw bullet holes appearing on his wings. An Albatros was on his tail. Relying on the same maneuver he used during his first kill, Bishop did a backward loop, dived at nearly two hundred miles per hour after the German, and opened fire at close range. The foe spiraled to his death.

In a repeat of what happened during his initial victory, the engine of his plane conked out again. *I have no choice but to land and give myself up,* he thought. He glided down, intending to strike a tree with one wing after landing so he could damage the plane without injuring himself and make it useless to the enemy.

As he neared the ground, he felt sick to his stomach. His thoughts turned to home, to his brother, sister, parents, and his fiancée, Margaret Eaton Burden, back in Canada. *They will feel heartbroken when they learn I've been captured — if they even find out.* His plane was now fifteen feet off the ground. *Poor Margaret, she —* Without any warning, the silent engine began to sputter, then cough. A few seconds later, it roared to life. "Wonderful! Wonderful!" he shouted. Skimming low over the terrain, he glanced over his shoulder and saw a cloud of smoke and flames coming from the balloon.

On his way back through enemy territory, Bishop deliberately flew close to the ground, knowing anti-aircraft weapons couldn't get him and that no pilot was crazy enough to dive at him at such a low altitude. Most of the German soldiers he buzzed were so startled to see him they either scattered, forgot to fire, or shot wildly. When he flew over three lines of German trenches, his plane took several bullets, but he made it back to his aerodrome without further trouble.

For shooting down his third plane and destroying a balloon, Bishop was given his first decoration — the Military Cross.

A few days later, on Easter Sunday, he was alone in the skies when he tangled with an Albatros again. The dogfight ended in a draw after his foe fled. But soon another German attacked him. The two dived and swooped at each other and fired dozens of rounds without scoring any hits. Then Bishop's gun jammed. While feverishly trying to fix it, the defenseless pilot kept dodging his adversary. After getting the weapon to work again, Bishop went after the Albatros with a vengeance. He maneuvered into a perfect position, blasted away, and sent the German plane tumbling out of control to a fiery crash.

His joy over the victory vanished when he now found himself dealing with five enemy aircraft, including one on his tail. Bullets ripped into his plane, and one grazed his leather-capped head. Bishop banked sharply and dealt with his attacker. Darting into position, he fired a direct hit on his foe and watched with great satisfaction as the German plane spun downward and slammed into pieces on the ground for another victory.

Two other planes veered off and didn't return to do battle, but two remained in the dogfight. Down to only forty rounds of ammunition, Bishop thought, *I either have to attack or be attacked. So attack!*

Banking, looping, and diving, he kept shooting until he ran out of ammo. Before he had to figure out his next move, the other two pilots called it quits and left. Thankful that he was the only one left in the sky, he headed for the aerodrome.

In honor of his five victories, which officially made Bishop an ace, his mechanic painted the aircraft's nose blue. Bishop was also promoted to captain.

The next four weeks became known as Bloody April, because the Royal Flying Corps suffered so many casualties that month. During one horrendous four-day stretch, seventy-five Allied aircraft and 105 airmen were lost in combat. Most of them were victims of Germany's Manfred von Richthofen — better known as the Red Baron — and his highly experienced, better-equipped pilots who made up his "Flying Circus." They were always easy to spot because their planes were painted a brilliant scarlet from nose to tail. In the majority of dogfights with these red birds, the Brits lost. In fact, the average flying life of an RFC pilot in the Arras region during the month was just eighteen hours.

Not so for Bishop. By the end of April, he had chalked up an amazing twenty victories — and on the last day of the month, he faced off against the Red Baron himself. Bishop and Major Alan Scott were flying side by side when they encountered von Richthofen and three of his Flying Circus planes. The major opened fire on the rear enemy plane from behind. Immediately, the Red Baron did a lightning-quick turn and blasted away at Scott, coming within two feet of him.

On one pass, Bishop got in three good bursts at the Baron but missed and was forced to spend the next few minutes on defense because he was getting attacked from every direction. Everywhere he turned, smoking bullets were zipping past him. Bishop couldn't see what was happening to Scott and wasn't at all certain what was going to happen to himself.

In the four-against-two dogfight, the planes whirled around one another like a tornado, barely avoiding numerous collisions. Bishop would catch a flash of silver as Scott would whizz by, but mostly he saw red streaks of the Flying

Circus. It was an incredibly fast-paced fight that Bishop had never experienced before.

To make things more hair-raising for Bishop, his gun jammed. Even though his plane was getting peppered with bullets, he managed to stay airborne. His weapon started firing again just seconds after he had the Red Baron in his sights. Bishop fired anyway, but it was too late as von Richthofen zoomed past him.

Bishop and Scott were fighting for their lives against the best pilots they had ever faced when unexpectedly four British Navy triplanes arrived, giving the Brits a six-to-four advantage. Now outnumbered, the Red Baron and his pilots sped off to fight another day.

When Bishop returned to the aerodrome, he examined his badly shot-up plane and saw that one grouping of seven bullets had struck the cockpit within an inch of his seat. "It was a close shave," Bishop told Scott, "but it was a wonder-ful, soul-stirring fight."

Close calls were nothing new for Bishop. After returning from one deadly dogfight, he discovered that his plane had more than two hundred bullet holes. Once, while attacking a pair of German two-seaters, his plane was hit in the engine by anti-aircraft fire. Leaving the dogfight, Bishop nursed the aircraft toward home, but the engine burst into flames and the fire spread to one wing. His burning plane crashed into a stand of poplar trees, leaving him unconscious and strapped upside down in the cockpit. As flames threatened to consume him and the plane, passing infantrymen rescued him in the nick of time.

In June and July, Bishop racked up dozens of victories. One of his best days was June 2, 1917, when he flew behind enemy lines at the crack of dawn and attacked a German airfield. While facing heavy ground fire, he shot down three planes as they tried to take off. Then he turned around and made it back home in time for breakfast. Although he came away unscathed, his plane had seventeen bullet holes and its fabric was torn and hanging from the wings.

By August, Bishop had become the highest-scoring ace in the RFC and was awarded the Victoria Cross for his heroism, the highest gallantry medal in the British Empire. Allowed a lengthy leave, Bishop returned to Canada in fall 1917, where he was given a hero's welcome and asked to speak at various functions to boost the morale of his fellow Canadians. He also used this time to marry his sweetheart, Margaret.

In April 1918, when the RFC became the Royal Air Force, Bishop was promoted to major and given command of No. 85 Squadron, known as the "Flying Foxes." The newly formed unit, whose pilots were handpicked by Bishop, flew faster, more agile S.E.5a biplanes out of an aerodrome in Petite-Synthe, France. Even though he was a commander, he considered himself a fighter pilot first, so he continued his deadly assault in the air, adding to his total of sixty-seven downed enemy aircraft.

But then on June 18 the Canadian government — worried that the country's morale would suffer if he were killed — ordered Bishop home to help organize the new Canadian Flying Corps. He didn't want to go, writing his wife, Margaret, "I've never been so furious in my life. It makes me livid with rage to be pulled away." But he had to follow orders, which stated that he must leave France by noon the following day. He figured that gave him time for one more solo mission.

Early the next morning, he flew over enemy territory south of Ypres, Belgium, looking for action — and found it. He was attacked by five Pfalz D.IIIa scouts — fast, single-seat biplanes with two mounted machine guns. Three of the planes dived on him, their guns sending tracers tearing through his lower left wingtip while he fired a short burst at them. As the trio zoomed past him, the other two Pfalz scouts dived at him from behind.

After making a sharp turn, Bishop opened fire and shot and killed one pilot whose plane then plummeted to the ground. While evading the two Germans who were blazing away at him from behind, Bishop chased after the first two planes that were trying to hide in a nearby cloud. He was closing in on them when, in their panic, the two German pilots collided. Both their planes broke apart in chunks of wood, metal, and fabric.

Concentrating now on the remaining two Pfalzes, Bishop saw they were climbing toward the safety of the clouds. He caught up with one of them and shot it down. The other German managed to escape.

But Bishop wasn't ready to quit. He continued to patrol the area, and his patience — or desire for more kills — paid off. He spotted a two-seat German reconnaissance plane. Flying behind and below it, Bishop raised the nose of his plane and fired lethal rounds into the belly of the enemy aircraft. It shuddered for a few seconds before plunging earthward and crashing in a ball of flames — the seventy-second aircraft to fall victim to Bishop's attacks. Only then, after recording a personal best of five victories in one day, which happened to come in the final hours of his career as a fighter pilot, did the Canadian hero head home.

It was a fitting — and astounding — end to the remarkable combat career of Billy Bishop, the Allies' ace of aces.

After the war, Bishop formed a small airline with fellow ace William Barker, but after legal and financial problems and a plane crash, the business eventually failed. He sold scrap metal in England before going into the oil business in Montreal, Quebec. During World War II, he was director of recruiting for the Royal Canadian Air Force. Bad health forced him to retire in 1952 with the rank of air marshal. Four years later, Bishop died in Palm Beach, Florida, at age sixty-two and was given a funeral with full military honors in Toronto.

His boyhood house in Owen Sound was turned into a museum and designated an historic sight. Canada's Air Command Headquarters in Winnipeg was named in his honor. His medals and other memorabilia were donated to the Canadian War Museum in Ottawa, Ontario.

Bishop's seventy-two victories ranks third among the top aces of World War I, behind Manfred "The Red Baron" von Richthofen with eighty and French pilot René Paul Fonck with seventy-five.

Von Richthofen was fatally wounded on April 21, 1918, during a low-level dogfight over Morlancourt Ridge in northern France. He had been shot in the heart.

Much of the source material for this story comes from Bishop's book Winged Warrior, which he wrote during the war.

THE "SUICIDE CLUB" HERO
Army Private John "Jack" Barkley

Sergeant Victor Nayhone stared into the eyes of Private John "Jack" Barkley and said, "The Germans occupy the woods on the other side of the valley at Cunel and the crest of Hill 253. We must find out what they are up to. Are they reinforcing the hill, or are they preparing a counterattack? We need you to take up a position overlooking the valley beyond Hill 253's northern slope and tell us what they're doing."

Barkley's orders called for him to slip behind enemy lines and set up a one-man observation post even though he would be dangerously exposed and well beyond any rescue should the Germans discover him. To the private, this sounded like a suicide mission. *I'll be going in an area crawling with Germans,* he thought. Mockingly, he told Nayhone,

"This is so crazy that maybe I should just go ask the Germans to give me the information."

"This is serious," Nayhone snapped. "We need that information."

"If you want to bump me off, for God's sake, do it here."

Ignoring the sarcasm, Nayhone said, "I know you'll do the best you can."

The private sighed and nodded. Shaking the sergeant's hand, he said, "All right. No hard feelings. But when you find my body, write a nice letter home to my folks."

Barkley knew the dangers he faced the moment he became a member of the "Suicide Club" — the ghoulish nickname given to the U.S. Army's field intelligence division. Operating near or behind enemy lines, he and his fellow soldiers who made up this stealth unit often worked alone or in pairs under the most perilous conditions. There was no margin for error, because few lived who made more than one mistake. Far too many never returned alive; thus, the grim moniker.

Barkley was good at his job. In fact, what he ended up doing on that hill was so remarkable he would eventually receive the prestigious Medal of Honor. And to think that he almost didn't get into the military solely because of the way he spoke.

"It's no use, Jack," said the recruiter. "There's no place in the army for a fellow who stutters as badly as you do." The recruiter, who was the postmaster in Jack's home town of Holden, Missouri, had known the young man his whole life.

Like other able-bodied men at the time, the twenty-two-year-old farmer's son had a bad case of "war fever" and wanted to enlist so he could fight for his country. He had been turned down earlier by an army recruiter because of his stuttering, but then he received a letter from the draft board requiring him to report for a physical for possible military service. Jack, who was fit and strong from working on the family farm, easily passed the physical before facing members of the draft board. When they peppered him with questions, he became so rattled that his stuttering went from bad to worse. At the end of the session, Jack asked, "D-d-did I-I-I p-p-pass?"

"No," a draft board member declared. "They'll never let you in the military."

But another member overruled him, claiming, "We're not picking orators. We're picking fighting men!"

Before embarking on the train that would take him to Camp Funston in Kansas for basic training, Barkley said good-bye to his dogs; his horse, Charley; and his parents. He didn't have many close friends because he spent most of his time out in the woods with a hunting rifle and his dogs. Out there it was easy to forget that everybody laughed at him when he tried to talk.

He experienced plenty of ribbing during basic training. But jokes about his stuttering dwindled after he was selected for training at Fort Riley, Kansas, for the army's intelligence service (the forerunner of today's Special Forces). He was trained to be a sniper and scout who operated behind enemy lines. He studied camouflage techniques and the tactics of the German Army, learned how to use the enemy's weapons, and developed skills in hand-to-hand fighting and long-range shooting.

Shipped to France, Barkley and his comrades received further training from French intelligence officers. He was trained to move with the slow, smooth precision of a wild animal stalking its prey. One quick movement would likely catch the eye of the enemy. As a sniper, he learned to lie perfectly still for several minutes, then set the telescopic sights, cock the rifle, and aim it with little motion of his arm before easing his finger on the trigger and firing. He was told how to take advantage of shadows because a glint of sun on the muzzle of his rifle or on the lens of his telescopic sight could alert the enemy. Instructors taught him how to find his way in the pitch-black without a compass and to walk silently in the forest and streams. To make himself blend into the background, he learned how to smear clay on his face, hands, and weapons and to fasten grass, weeds, and burlap to his clothing.

By summer 1918, Barkley was on a troop train that was taking members of the 4th Infantry, 3rd Division to their first combat experience. During a stop, he and his comrades were stunned by what they saw through the windows of a passing French hospital train that was returning from the front. The cars were packed with the wounded, some screaming in pain, some lying near death, some shaking from the effects of poison gas.

As the hospital train slowly rumbled by, Barkley and the other new soldiers watched quietly in horror. Finally, someone broke the silence and said, "If it's as bad as I think it is at the front, we better shoot those Germans mighty quick."

"I–I–I a-a-a-gr-gr-gree," Barkley uttered.

Trying to lighten the mood, his buddy, a Cherokee and fellow private named Jesse James, cracked, "Shooting? Why, Jack, you couldn't hit a flock of barns!"

Of course, everyone in the unit knew that Barkley was a superb marksman who excelled in hitting targets from long distances. But no one, including Barkley himself, knew how he would do under live combat conditions. He was days away from finding out.

When the troops got off the train at Montmirail in northeastern France, the tension of war was ratcheted up by the steady stream of French refugees trudging into town. The people, who had left their homes from the invading Germans, hardly glanced up at the Americans. *They have dead looks on their faces,* Barkley thought. *It's as if they can't see anything or feel anything anymore.* This sad consequence of the war caused his stomach to churn.

He and his comrades in the intelligence service were soon given their first mission: sneak out in pairs and secretly establish observation posts close to the enemy lines near Château Thierry and report back on the Germans' movements.

Besides the regular equipment, Barkley carried a telescopic sight for his rifle, binoculars, pistol, twenty pounds of ammunition, canteen, and gas mask. He teamed up with Mike De Angelo, a runner who delivered messages. They trekked up a hill where enemy snipers lay hidden and headed toward the sound of guns. For months Barkley had heard about, thought about, and lived nothing but the war. Now he was ready to experience it firsthand.

After reaching the edge of a cliff, he and De Angelo settled in a clump of brush overlooking the river valley near Château Thierry. Off to the left on the crest of the hill, the men of the 9th Machine Gun Battalion were crouched behind rocks firing down on the German columns that were marching toward the river.

Through his high-powered binoculars, Barkley saw that many of the Germans were marching to certain death as they neared the bridges. Turning his gaze to the wooded hill opposite the American machine gunners, he spotted four German artillery batteries setting up about a mile away. They were aiming their cannons at the Americans.

"The Germans will blow the top of our boys' hill to pieces!" Barkley declared. "We've got to stop them!" His fingers trembling, he wrote down the position of the enemy batteries and handed them to De Angelo. "For God's sake, Mike, take this and beat it!" As the runner took off in a sprint, Barkley thought, *I wonder how long it'll take the Germans to get their shells in range of our hilltop.*

If his message didn't arrive in time for the Americans to destroy those four batteries, the enemy artillery would pummel the U.S. machine gunners. Soon the Germans' big guns roared and shells began exploding closer and closer to their target. *Did Mike make it back to headquarters?* Barkley wondered. *It'll only be minutes before the Germans wipe out our guys.* Just then, American artillery sprang into action and, using the coordinates that Barkley had given, destroyed the enemy's big guns in time.

Over the next several weeks, Barkley crept behind enemy lines to gather vital information, killed German officers with his long-range shooting skills as a sniper, dealt with gas attacks, and was wounded during hand-to-hand combat. He became a veteran soldier in no time.

One day, Barkley had just finished talking on a field phone from his observation post when an enemy artillery shell exploded only thirty feet away. Shrapnel slammed through the branches, smashed the phone, and came within an inch of slicing his hand. The force of the blast left him unconscious and somewhat buried under dirt, rock, and branches. After regaining consciousness, he wriggled out of the debris, put on his gas mask, and made his way back to headquarters.

Reporting to an officer, Barkley said, "If I hadn't been knocked out, I would've been back a lot sooner." The way he talked sounded strange to him. And then it dawned on him: *I just spoke without stuttering for the first time in my life!*

Wondering if his brain was playing tricks on him because of the explosion, Barkley went up to his friend Jesse James and launched into a brief monologue.

"My God," James said, "what's gotten into you? You're talking like a human being!"

Barkley never stuttered again.

During the latter two weeks of September, his unit was on the move as the big guns roared and rifles barked all night and all day. Barkley and his comrades were getting weak with hunger and lack of sleep, but still they kept advancing with no chance to bathe or shave.

In early October, the Americans drove the Germans from Woods 268 — ground near the French town of Montfaucon that the enemy had held for more than a year. However, German artillery fire grew increasingly accurate and deadly by the time Barkley's battalion was ordered to take Woods 250. Because it would be close fighting, Barkley exchanged his rifle for a sawed-off shotgun and packed a pistol, thirty-five rounds of ammo in clips, a trench knife, and two grenades.

That night, the battalion attacked, triggering fierce hand-to-hand combat. Although he was slightly built, Barkley was a scrappy, experienced fighter from his school days when he used his fists to silence taunts about his stuttering. But in war, it was life or death. Before killing one particular foe, he was stabbed in the leg by a bayonet.

A few days later, Barkley was summoned by Sergeant

Nayhone, who briefed him on a dangerous scouting mission that the private was convinced would be suicidal. The Germans held the crest of Hill 253, while the Americans controlled the slope on the southern side. Across the valley, the Germans also occupied the woods by the village of Cunel.

"No one can see into the valley behind Hill 253," Nayhone explained. "Our pilots can't tell what the Germans are doing because of the rain. Someone has to go in No Man's Land and take up a position overlooking the valley beyond Hill 253's northern slope. That someone is you."

After putting up a sarcastic protest, Barkley headed out into the night with two signalmen who carried a phone and laid wire in an area infested with Germans. After following the ridge line for two hours, Barkley settled in a shell hole of an area that had been the scene of intense fighting earlier. The signalmen gave him the phone, which was set to buzz lightly and not ring, and then left.

Barkley called Nayhone, who told him, "Don't talk. You're too close to the Germans and they might hear you. Just report to me in code by scratching your mouthpiece with your fingernail."

Physically, Barkley couldn't have been more uncomfortable. He was up to his knees in mud and gagging from the stench of the dead bodies that were sprawled all over the ground. *There's nothing to keep a sniper from discovering I'm here,* he thought. But he was so exhausted that he stopped worrying about it.

By morning, October 7, 1918, he saw that the Germans were getting ready to cross the valley and launch a counterattack, so he immediately phoned Nayhone with the development.

In the early afternoon, Barkley was giving his latest report to Nayhone when the German heavy artillery opened on American-held Woods 250 and the southern slope of Hill 253.

"Stay there as long as you can," Nayhone told him. "Take care of yourself. If anything —" The phone went dead.

Shell fire must have cut the line, Barkley thought. As he mulled over his next move, he noticed a small two-man French tank that had been abandoned during the earlier fighting. The lightweight tank, a Renault FT-17, was in a perfect strategic position to create havoc against the German assault. *Imagine what I could do if I had a machine gun in that tank,* Barkley thought. *But there are seventy-five yards of open ground between me and the tank, and the sun is shining straight down on the ridge, so it'll be easy for the enemy to spot me.* He shelved the idea. *It's too dangerous.*

There were usually plenty of guns left behind on the battlefield, but the Germans made a practice of throwing away each breechblock — a vital part of the firing mechanism — from their dead comrades so their foes couldn't use the weapons. Without the breechblock, the gun was useless. However, Barkley had learned about the workings of the German guns during intelligence service training and had been carrying a breechblock for weeks to use in just such a situation.

He spotted a light Maxim machine gun and a few boxes of ammunition among a group of dead Germans near the edge of the woods. *If I can get hold of the Maxim and some ammo without being picked off by a sniper, I can make things interesting for a while,* he thought.

The German force of about six hundred was beginning to move along the edge of their side of the woods. He noticed they were Jagers — a good fighting outfit made up of strong, heavyset men in their thirties. They were carrying grenades, heavy and light machine guns, and plenty of ammunition.

Barkley slipped out from his hiding place and dashed over to the Maxim. Just as he was about to pick it up, American artillery opened up on the woods with shells that exploded in a smoke screen, effectively providing him with cover from the enemy for the next several minutes.

He grabbed the gun and all the ammunition he could carry and raced for the baby tank. Once he climbed inside, he examined the Maxim and found it was in excellent condition except for a missing breechblock. He pulled out the breechblock that he had been carrying, snapped it into the gun, and tested it. *It works!*

He jumped outside and, with one eye on the smoke screen, gathered up all the ammunition he could find from the bodies of the dead Germans. Back in the tank, he stuck the barrel of the Maxim out the firing port, inserted a belt of shells, and turned the turret so that the gun was pointing toward the German-held woods.

As the smoke screen thinned out and the air became clear again, he caught a glimpse of movement at the edge of the woods. The Germans were cautiously coming out into the open in formation and moving diagonally across his front toward the crest of Hill 253. He turned the turret slowly to keep pace with their progress and waited until those in the rear had left the woods and started up the slope. There was no cover in the open field for most of them. *I have them right where I want them,* he told himself.

He took a long breath, aimed, and squeezed the trigger. His ambush momentarily stunned the Germans as they huddled together, frantically looking in every direction for the source of the bullets. Taking advantage of their confusion, Barkley fired burst after burst. When he finished the first belt of ammo, he jammed in the next one. But the gun began to act up so he fired a little slower.

When the Germans discovered the source of the shooting, they fired back. Their bullets beat a steady tattoo on the little tank, but Barkley knew they couldn't do any harm — unless some lucky rounds came through the open firing port. Because the tank was cone-shaped, the bullets tended to bounce off or shatter into fragments. The noise inside, however, was deafening.

Within minutes, the Germans on the slope had pointed their machine guns in Barkley's direction. The gunfire against the tank was so heavy Barkley wondered if it would melt. It sounded as if a thousand hammers were battering the sides.

He stopped firing every few minutes to let his gun cool off and to open up boxes of ammunition. When the water-cooled Maxim began to smoke, he poured water from his canteen into the weapon's water jacket, but the steam it caused nearly scalded his face and hands. Barkley recovered quickly and kept swinging his weapon between the Germans on the hill and those in the woods. One soldier fired a burst squarely at the tank's gun port, sending two bullets inside, but neither struck Barkley.

Eventually, an enemy patrol of about twenty, carrying two light Maxims and many grenades, scrambled from shell hole to shell hole toward the tank. He managed to kill some of them, but the rest set up their weapons about seventy-five yards away. The Germans in the woods opposite them ceased firing so they wouldn't hit their own patrol.

One soldier with a Maxim started firing straight at the barrel of Barkley's gun, trying to destroy it. Barkley whirled the turret toward him, fired, and shot him. Meanwhile, the rest of the patrol crawled up closer and began flinging grenades at the tank, which did little damage. They needed to get closer — something Barkley was determined wouldn't happen.

Soon, though, an enemy artillery shell burst nearby. Then another landed closer, followed by a third that was even nearer. He swung the turret to look for the big gun. On the fourth shot, he spotted the flash from the weapon. It was a field gun — a 77-mm cannon on two wheels hidden in the edge of the woods at the far end of the valley about six hundred yards away.

Before he could get his sights placed, a shell exploded next to the tank with an earsplitting boom and concussion that knocked him out. He awoke a few minutes later, struggling for breath and bleeding from his nose. The air was thick and smoky.

Realizing that the bullets had stopped beating against the tank, he threw open the turret door, stuck his head out, and took some deep breaths. Then he saw why there were no more bullets coming his way.

The German troops had reformed on the slope of Hill 253 and were advancing toward the crest. But they were being met by deadly fire from machine guns that the Americans had set up while the Germans were busy dealing with Barkley. *The Germans thought that fifth shell put me out of the game because they're not even watching the tank now,* he thought. Their dead were piled thick everywhere on the slope in front of him.

Barkley went back inside the tank and closed the door. Then he swung the turret until he relocated the field gun. He didn't know if his weapon would shoot at such a long range, but he was going to try — even though it meant that the Germans would realize that he wasn't hurt and that the tank wasn't out of commission.

Relying on his skill as a long-range shooter, he unloaded an entire belt aimed at the field gun and disabled it. But his success forced the Germans to turn their attention back to him. Once again, they fired at the tank with their rifles and machine guns. Barkley continued to swing his weapon back and forth, spraying the woods on his right and the slope of Hill 253 on his left.

To his dismay, his gun began to jam until it worked only as a single-shot weapon. *I've come to the end of my rope,* he thought. Bullets were spattering against the tank from all sides. *They can't send a patrol out for me as long as that keeps up. But neither can I get out of the tank and make a break for the woods. Yet that's the only option I have.* As he crawled to the driver's side, he found a can of thin oil. He filled the gun with the oil, thrust the barrel out through the firing port, and pulled the trigger. The Maxim returned to life. *I'm still in the game!*

He felt better — until seconds later when a grenade burst against the turret. Peering out the port, he saw that an enemy patrol had moved considerably closer to the tank, so he fired short bursts at them, forcing them to dive into nearby shell holes. He noticed that one of the Germans dropped a big bag of grenades on the ground right outside a crater. Barkley took careful aim and fired at the bag. It exploded with enough force to shake the tank and wound several of the enemy. The uninjured foes sprinted back to the safety of the woods.

Barkley continued to stymie the German attack until the Maxim began to overheat again and burned up all the oil. By now the tank inside stunk so badly he could hardly breathe, and the thick smoke around the gun made it difficult to see out the port. The gun sputtered and finally quit. He was nearly out of ammunition anyway.

I'll wait for the gun to cool off, he thought. *Who am I kidding? It's really the end I'm waiting for. I can't hold out much longer with a gun that fires only once in a while.* He didn't even bother to look out for enemy patrols anymore. *If they're coming, they're coming. There's nothing much I can do about it except kill a few before they kill me.* He checked to make sure the two pistols he carried were functioning. Then he sat there, sick to his stomach and with his head in his hands, waiting for his doom.

Suddenly, he heard booms of a different kind. He swung the turret around and saw that shells from American artillery were bursting all over the slope of Hill 253. Supported by the artillery, troops from the 30th Infantry were advancing from Woods 250 in pursuit of the Germans who were running like rabbits for their own woods on the opposite side of the valley. Behind the enemy, soldiers from the 7th Infantry were sweeping down from the top of Hill 253.

Barkley threw open the tank door and climbed out. As an American platoon passed, its officer asked him, "What company do you belong to, soldier?"

"Company K, of the 4th Infantry, sir."

"What the devil are you doing over here?"

"I've been holding the fort in that tank, sir."

The officer stared at the tank, peeked inside it, and then looked at Barkley and said, "You look terrible. Now go find out where your outfit is and rejoin them!"

Barkley saluted and started off toward Woods 250 while the officer and platoon continued their pursuit of the Germans. About a minute later, Barkley heard a loud roar from behind. He turned around and saw that a six-inch shell from a German heavy artillery gun had exploded just a few feet from the tank. As he stumbled through the woods he heard more shells crashing all around the tank. *The Germans finally found the range of the tank — too late.*

When he arrived at battalion headquarters, he reported to Sergeant Nayhone, who threw his arms around Barkley and said, "You got back after all, Jack!"

"Of course," Barkley replied. "I'm not good-looking enough to be an angel."

For single-handedly harassing an enemy advance, Barkley was awarded the Medal of Honor during a military ceremony in vanquished Germany several months after the enemy had surrendered. What was so remarkable about the presentation was that Barkley had no idea that he was being awarded the medal.

During the ceremony, in which other soldiers were being decorated for bravery with lesser medals, General John "Black Jack" Pershing pinned the Medal of Honor on Barkley's chest. But the soldier still didn't know what it was. Not until he looked down and saw that the medal had stars and a blue ribbon did he realize he was the newest recipient of the prestigious award.

After Barkley returned to civilian life, he got married and ran a dairy farm in Johnson County, Kansas. He later became the first superintendent of the county's park and recreation district. Barkley wrote a book about his life in the military, No Hard Feelings!, which is the main source for this story. (Years later, the book was rewritten by editors and re-titled and re-released as Scarlet Fields: The Combat Memoir of a World War I Medal of Honor Hero.)

He died in 1966 at the age of seventy-one and is buried in Forest Hill Cemetery in Kansas City, Missouri.

THE POW ESCAPEE
Navy Lieutenant Edouard Izac

O n the morning of May 31, 1918, the Navy troopship USS *President Lincoln* was returning from France after completing its fifth successful transatlantic voyage, having delivered five thousand American troops and eight thousand tons of cargo.

Navy Lieutenant Edouard Izac stood on the deck of the steamer and inhaled the brisk salt air. Since leaving the port of Brest the day before with thirty injured soldiers, the ship had been in a convoy escorted by two destroyers through the most dangerous section of the Atlantic where German submarines, known as U-boats, lurked. But now, seemingly out of danger, the vessel was all alone.

The twenty-six-year-old Iowa-born officer gazed at the rolling waves and thought, *What a beautiful morning*.

Suddenly, the ship was rocked by a violent explosion, and

then another, both near the bow. Izac and his fellow sailors instantly rushed to their battle stations. As he ran toward the stern, another blast shook the vessel, showering him with saltwater. *Torpedoes!* he thought.

From his battle station near the stern, he saw the periscope of an enemy sub about eight hundred yards ahead of the *President Lincoln* off the port bow. A sense of pride swept over him as the sailors were carrying out their duties flawlessly and firing the ship's four guns with precision and discipline. Most of the 685 sailors had less than a year's experience on the high seas and many had never even seen an ocean-going ship, let alone manned one, before joining the Navy.

Ten minutes after the ship was struck, a messenger raced up to Izac and shouted above the din, "Holds Number Five and Six are flooded, and water is approaching Number One deck!"

Izac felt his stomach tighten. *This is bad.* He relayed the dire news to the captain, Percy Foote, who had received similar reports from others. And then Izac heard the words that all sailors fear the most: "Abandon ship!" the captain ordered.

Under Izac's directions, all hands in the stern were off the vessel in lifeboats and on rafts within five minutes. Izac remained onboard until waves began lapping over the main deck. Then he jumped into a life raft and ordered everyone to row away from the sinking ship.

Thirty minutes later, the *President Lincoln* turned over gently to starboard, put her bow in the air, and slipped stern first under the surface. As the debris-filled waters closed over her, Izac stood up and shouted, "Three cheers for the *President Lincoln*, the best ship that ever carried troops in the cause of freedom!" Tears welled in his eyes as the men shouted, "Hip, hip, hooray! Hip, hip, hooray! Hip, hip, hooray!"

After a head count revealed that all but twenty-six had survived, the crew secured the rafts to the lifeboats so they wouldn't be scattered over the ocean. Shortly after Izac jumped from his raft into a lifeboat, the enemy submarine surfaced, revealing its identity — the U-90.

"Lieutenant," said one of Izac's men, "hide under the sail. When they find out you're an officer, they're going to take you prisoner." Other crewmen agreed and pleaded with him to hide or at least take off his officer's uniform.

I can't bring myself to the humiliation of hiding in the bottom of the lifeboat, Izac told himself. Although he lost his officer's cap and he was wearing a life jacket, it was obvious to the approaching Germans that he was indeed an officer.

The commanding officer of the U-boat put a megaphone to his lips and ordered Izac, "Come aboard!" The lifeboat pulled alongside, and as Izac rose to step onto the submarine, his men protested and tried to restrain him, because he faced an unknown fate. They, on the other hand, knew they would get picked up by nightfall by two American destroyers that were already steaming to their rescue after having received distress calls. Izac told his sailors, "Don't worry. It's only the fortunes of war. I will be fine and so will you." He forced a smile, shook hands with those closest to him, and hopped onto the deck of the submarine.

After taking Izac's pistol, a German sailor led him to the conning tower where the American saluted the sub's captain. In rather fair English, the captain asked, "Are you the captain of the *President Lincoln*?"

"No, sir," Izac replied. "I believe the captain went down with the ship, for I have not seen him since," he lied. Izac knew that Captain Foote had taken off his uniform and was in a lifeboat in charge of keeping the survivors safe. "I am Edouard Izac, the first lieutenant."

"I am Captain Walter Remy," the German said. "My orders are to take the senior officer prisoner whenever I sink a man-o'-war."

Although he was a POW now, Izac was treated with respect and dignity by Remy and the German officers, who all spoke broken English. In fact, the American ate, drank coffee, and even played cards with them.

The next afternoon, Izac was chatting with Remy in the wardroom when an officer announced, "Two American destroyers have spotted us!"

As the crewmen rushed to their stations, the U-90 quickly submerged to a depth of more than two hundred feet and began zigzagging, trying to lose its pursuers. Left alone in the wardroom, Izac was filled with mixed feelings — hope that the destroyers would sink the sub and fear that they actually would.

A few minutes later, a dull concussion made the U-boat wobble. *It's a depth bomb!* Izac thought. Other blasts followed, including five that exploded so close the sub shook violently from bow to stern. Izac, who eventually counted twenty-two depth charge blasts, fully expected that at any second the seams of the U-boat's steel plates would split open and water would gush in, drowning all hands, including him. But the sub held together and soon the sound of the destroyers' propellers grew fainter. An hour later, the U-90 surfaced in a calm sea.

"The depth bombs are bad, and that's part of the business," Remy told Izac. "But what I dread the most is passing through unknown mine fields."

Even though he was treated surprisingly well, Izac told himself, *I must find a way to escape.* When no one was looking, he searched lockers, hoping to find something to aid him in either capturing the submarine or escaping from it. There was nothing.

However, the officers continued to treat him more like a visitor than a prisoner, so he used that to his advantage. He made detailed mental notes of the U-90's route and how and where it had slipped past Allied ships. He paid close attention to enemy maneuvers along the northern German coast and the warships in the busy harbors. He gathered a wealth of intelligence that he knew would be of extreme importance to the Allied cause. *I must escape!* he told himself.

The U-90 docked in Wilhelmshaven, the base of the German High Seas Fleet, as a patrolling zeppelin circled overhead. Izac counted twenty-five destroyers and seven battleships in the harbor, which was bustling with repair ships, tugs, and transports. Remy said good-bye to Izac, who was taken away, interrogated by gruff officers, and treated harshly. When Izac didn't give up any information, he was shipped by train, under armed guard, to a prison in Karlsruhe in southwestern Germany.

The prison camp was made up of wooden shacks in the middle of a courtyard and was surrounded by an inner seven-foot-tall wire fence, then a twelve-foot-high wooden fence topped by barbed wire, and an outer wire fence. Sentries were spaced about thirty yards apart along the perimeter. The camp held about one hundred British, sixty French, fifteen Italian, and five Serbian officers, many of them nursing war wounds. They were given little food or medical attention. Izac realized that his treatment aboard the U-90 was far from the norm for a POW.

"I've gathered valuable intelligence about the German Navy, and I need to tell my superiors," Izac told the Brits. "I must escape to Switzerland."

So Izac and six other POWs planned an escape. Working late every night, they loosened the staples that held the wires of the inner fence to the posts so they could make an opening large enough to pass through. They also unscrewed a board in the middle fence. Bribing a friendly guard, one of the prisoners, a French aviator, smuggled out a letter to friends in Karlsruhe asking them to hide the escapees for a few days.

To help the seven men, fellow prisoners donated money they had sewn in their clothes before their capture and gave them food from Red Cross packages. Izac jammed a compass deep in a jar of lard, concealed money in a container of shaving cream, and fashioned a knapsack out of a shirt that held maps and food.

For patriotic reasons, Izac chose the night of the Fourth of July as the date to escape. But on the afternoon of July 3, the friendly guard was frisked at the main gate and found to be carrying a second letter to the French aviator's friends. The French prisoner was taken away and beaten and questioned. Although he refused to name the prisoners who were involved, the escape attempt failed.

Undeterred, Izac came up with a new scheme. But before he could implement it, he was put on a train with thirty other POWs for a prison in Villingen, a town in the Black Forest about one hundred miles south. Among the armed guards in the train were two who were a few feet away from him. The window near his seat was partially opened. *That's just enough space for me to squeeze through,* he told himself. *I'm sure I can reach it in one bound.* His muscles tensed as he waited for his opportunity. And then it came. One of the guards had dozed off while the other turned his head slightly to talk to someone else.

Now! With his makeshift knapsack hanging from his neck, Izac leaped past both guards and dived right through the window of the moving train. He landed hard on a railway bed of crushed rock, and his head struck a rail on a parallel set of tracks, stunning him. By the time the train stopped about three hundred yards away, he had cleared his senses. But he was battered and bruised, and his knees were so seriously injured that he couldn't run. As he tried shuffling away, the guards began shooting at him. Falling in pain from his injuries, he dragged himself, but stopped when a shot whizzed by his ear. Sickened with disappointment, he sat up and raised his hands above his head. "I surrender," he said.

With fiendish fury, a guard flipped his rifle around and grasped it by the muzzle. Swinging it like a baseball bat, he clubbed Izac in the head, knocking him out. When Izac regained consciousness, the guards cursed and kicked him. Every time they picked him up, they struck him with their fists and the butts of their weapons. They were enraged because if Izac had escaped, they would have spent at least two weeks in solitary confinement and then be sent to the trenches.

Prodding him with their bayonets, they forced Izac to limp the remaining five miles to Villingen. Barely conscious and in agony, the captive stumbled to the ground every time he was struck from behind, which was often. *I refuse to die,* he told himself. *I must bear my cross like a man. Oh, God, grant me the privilege of being an instrument of your vengeance against the Germans.*

Then he passed out. When he woke up, he was tied to a bed, staring at the fuming commandant, who was scream-ing at him in German. An interpreter told Izac, "He says if you try to escape again, you will be shot." A young man, who had been drafted from medical college to help the German war effort, treated Izac's wounds. "You'll live," the medic said, and then added, ". . . to be hanged."

The guards went through his knapsack and found the compass and money, but not the map. They also tore open all the seams of his clothes and ripped off the soles and heels of his shoes. Finding nothing more, they gave up the search.

As punishment, Izac was put in solitary confinement for two weeks. Since his initial capture on the high seas, Izac had lost thirty pounds and was a shell of his former self. *I will surely escape the next time*, he vowed to himself.

The prison held about one hundred and fifty Russians, most of whom were gaunt and withered, and forty Americans. Because he was the highest-ranking officer in the camp, Izac was made the leader. While trying to improve living conditions against disease-causing fleas, hunger, and his captors' cruelty, he kept plotting ways to escape the camp. In the previous four years, more than fifty prisoners had escaped from Villingen camp, mostly by digging tunnels. But Izac rejected that idea. Only one escapee had made it safely to nearby Switzerland, a neutral country. Besides, construction of a tunnel would take several months, and he didn't have the luxury of time. The German newspapers were boasting that U-boats were sinking ten thousand tons of Allied shipping daily. If that was true — and Izac hoped it was nothing but propaganda — then every day that he remained in prison without getting vital information to his superiors meant further losses for the Allies.

About a dozen Americans joined him in this latest escape effort. Using slats from under their beds, they secretly built ladders. They stole screws by unfastening one from each barrack door hinge. The plan called for the Russian prisoners to cause a commotion in a far corner of the prison. The Americans would plunge the camp into darkness by throwing chains of stolen metal wire, which Izac had fashioned, onto the bare electric wires that connected the lights around the perimeter, shorting them out. Then the escapees would use one of the makeshift ladders to get onto the roof of the work shed. At a given signal, they would jump down to another roof, use another ladder to climb the wire fence, and hop down on the outside.

By the middle of August, they were ready. They agreed to split in groups of two or three once they made it out of the camp. Izac teamed up with Harold Willis, an American pilot who flew for the French in the Lafayette Escadrille until he was shot down and captured a year earlier.

But during an inspection of one of the barracks, the guards discovered several hidden compasses and maps and noticed that some of the beds were missing slats. Once again, Izac's escape plan went up in smoke. It was a severe blow to him, and for the first time, he felt discouraged. "I lived a lifetime of hope and fear in the making of each one of those escape plans," Izac confided to Willis. "And to see them fail one by one is truly disheartening."

Conditions at Villingen turned much worse after the search. The prisoners were watched so closely that every plan Izac made was uncovered before it could be put into effect, plunging him deeper in despair. Later that summer, he received his first letter from home. It was from his wife, Agnes, whom he had married the day after he graduated from the United States Naval Academy. "We want you home for Christmas," she wrote him. *Somehow, some way I will be there for Christmas,* he vowed.

With new enthusiasm, Izac came up with another plan. When all was ready, thirteen Americans put on whatever clothes they had that made them look like civilians. Izac stuffed maps in a coat pocket and a compass and pepper (to be used to hinder tracking dogs) in another. He filled other pockets with French biscuits, sausage, and chocolate.

Late at night, they quickly assembled a wooden "bridge" that was eighteen feet long and eighteen inches wide from material they had stolen earlier. With a smuggled tool, they cut through an iron window grate in their barracks. One of the prisoners tossed the chain that Izac had made over the bare electrical wires and shorted out the lights. As he waited to make his move, Izac heard a ruckus in the far corner of the prison yard. *Right on cue,* he thought. The Russians were pretending to fight, drawing several guards in a diversion.

The escapees shoved their makeshift bridge out the window until it spanned the fifteen feet between the barrack window ledge and the top of the outer wall. As Izac, Willis, and the others crawled across it, the guards shouted, "Halt! Halt!" Dropping to the ground, Izac ran right past the outside sentries, who began firing wildly into the night. After one bullet nearly grazed his head, he doubled over and scrambled up an embankment three hundred yards away with Willis.

They scampered over hills, across streams, and through swamps during the night. At times, they were in water up to their shoulders. But even on dry ground, it wasn't easy going because their soggy clothes weighed them down and restricted their legs. They avoided roads and walked only in forests and fields. Instead of going across bridges, they forded or swam across the water. They never coughed or sneezed and seldom talked except in a whisper. Because it was so dark, they kept stumbling over tree roots, rocks, and holes. Occasionally, they stopped to cover their trail with pepper, then doubled back and jumped as far as possible off to the side to throw the dogs off their scent. When entering a brook, the pair slogged in the middle downstream for hundreds of yards before exiting on the opposite side in a further effort to thwart tracking.

The next morning, they climbed down a rocky cliff and camped in a thicket near a village about twelve miles from the prison. Exhausted, they took turns getting in a two-hour nap. At about 1 o'L . Izac and Willis became frazzled with anxiety by the distant baying of hounds that grew louder by the minute. "To flee now in broad daylight would only attract the attention of the villagers," Izac whispered. "Let's stay put, but be ready to move if we have to." The dread of discovery had jangled their already-raw nerves. But soon they heard the barks and howls turning to whines. "The dogs have lost our trail at the cliff," said Izac. "We're safe for now."

Night after night, they trekked onward, surviving on cabbages, potatoes, turnips, and other vegetables that they had swiped from farm fields. Every morning the fatigued men would find a place to hide and fall into a deep sleep. Because it was always cold, they huddled together under Willis's raincoat. The physical agony was bad enough; the mental strain was even worse, because they feared at any moment they would be captured.

On the seventh night of their escape, they came to the edge of a sheer cliff over the Rhine River, which separated Germany from Switzerland. For the first time in a week, Izac felt confident. *We're almost there!* They took off their coats, hats, and shoes and buried them. Then they covered their hands, faces, and clothes with dirt to darken them. Below them, they could hear the German sentries marching back and forth.

Because Izac and Willis couldn't find a safe way to climb down, they decided to crawl on their hands and knees in the middle of a mountain stream that flowed into the river. The cold water chilled them to the bone, and the rocks cut up their legs and feet during their two-hour torturous route. They knew that sentries were always just a few yards away, and a single misstep would mean capture — or death.

While the two were sneaking under a viaduct patrolled by guards, Willis winced from slamming his bare foot on a sharp rock. He was just loud enough to catch the guards' attention. A searchlight scanned the stream while Willis and Izac remained motionless with only their muddied heads above the water. The guards were too far away to notice the darkened faces, which blended in with the rock, and soon turned off the light, allowing the escapees to move on.

Shortly after 2 A.M. Izac and Willis reached the frigid, fast-flowing Rhine. "How far do you think it is across?" Izac whispered as they stepped into the water. Willis didn't respond. To Izac's shock, his buddy had disappeared in an instant even though he had been no more than a foot away. *What happened to him?* Izac thought. *Where did he go?* Fighting a bout of panic, Izac quickly stripped off his pants. But he lost his balance and found himself being carried off by the strong current toward the center of the river.

Izac was moving downstream at such a fast clip that he couldn't make any headway toward the Swiss side. Stroking furiously, he tried to break free from the current's grip. But the cold water, the lack of proper food and sleep, and the dozens of miles of walking had sapped most of his strength.

He kept fighting the current and then gave one final extra effort. It was just enough to push him closer to the Swiss side. But that desperate exertion had taken the last bit of energy out of him. *I can't do it anymore,* he thought. *I'm too weak.* He turned over on his back and, with his legs pointed downstream, floated helplessly. *I entrust my soul to you, God.* Then he closed his eyes. Seconds later, he felt his feet touch the rocks of the shoreline. He was in Switzerland.

Izac crawled out of the water and lay on the bank, gasping for breath and trying to find words for a proper thanksgiving. After five failed attempts to rise, he dragged himself to the top of the sloping shoreline. Standing on his cut-up feet and shivering in the howling wind, Izac thought, *I'm free at last! I have nothing to fear anymore!*

He staggered a short distance to a house, knocked on the door, and introduced himself as an escaped American prisoner. The owner, a Swiss customs guard, fed him and clothed him and gave him a place to sleep. The man also found Willis, who stumbled into a small tavern about two miles away. Willis explained that when he had stepped into the river to take his pants off, the current had swept him away. He couldn't yell to Izac because that would have alerted the sentries. He, too, had fought a difficult battle with the current while trying to get across the Rhine.

Izac and Willis were taken to the American embassy in Berne, where they were provided proper papers. They also learned that besides them, only one of the thirteen escapees had so far reached Switzerland.

Izac rushed to London and gave a detailed report of the intelligence he had gathered about the German Navy. A month later, enemy submarines and war ships returned to their home ports under the white flag. Germany had surrendered.

Izac arrived in the United States on November 11, 1918 — the very day the Armistice was signed between the Allies and Germany, effectively ending active combat in Europe.

Earlier, Willis had returned to active duty on the Western Front for the final month of the conflict. After the war, the Harvard graduate became an architect known for designing school buildings and churches. When World War II broke out, he enlisted in the United States Air Force and served as a major in Africa, England, and France. He died in 1962 at the age of seventy-two, leaving behind a wife, two sons, and six grandchildren.

Izac received several combat awards. For his resolve in escaping and delivering vital intelligence to naval authorities, Izac was awarded the Medal of Honor.

Moving to San Diego, California, he worked as a journalist after writing a memoir of his war days, Prisoner of U-90, which was the major source material for this story. From 1937 to 1947, he served in the United States House of Representatives before settling in the Washington, D.C., area, where he raised cattle. He had five children, nineteen grandchildren, and twenty-five great-grandchildren when he died in 1990 at the age of ninety-eight. At the time of his death, Izac, who is buried in Arlington National Cemetery, was the last living Medal of Honor recipient from World War I.

THE BATTLEFIELD SAVIOR

Ambulance Driver James "Jim" McConnell

Gripping the steering wheel of his Model T ambulance, James "Jim" McConnell looked behind at the three seriously wounded soldiers lying on bloody stretchers in the back. The men had been mangled by shrapnel from a German grenade and were hovering near death.

Every second counts, McConnell told himself. So he opened the throttle on the engine and headed toward the nearest hospital ten miles away in the village of Pont-à-Mousson in war-ravaged northeastern France. Suddenly, twenty yards in front of him, an enemy artillery shell exploded, sending up a geyser of mud and dirt that pelted his vehicle. He swerved to his left and kept going when another shell landed even closer, bursting only a few yards behind him and hurtling shards of hot metal.

Dodging shell craters and debris in the road, the American driver ignored the ground-shaking bombardment. His focus was to speed these casualties to a surgeon in the hospital so they had a fighting chance at life. He remembered what a medic at the front lines had told him when he braved the shelling to pick up the three wounded men: "If you can get them to the operating room quickly, maybe, just maybe, they can pull through. Jim, you must hurry!"

In the desperate rush for life, the ambulance swayed side to side on the rough road. He knew the bouncing and jarring were badly shaking the men in the back and causing them pain, but he didn't dare slow down.

As the ambulance sped through a demolished village, McConnell's main worry wasn't so much the shelling all around him, because he was used to it. He was concerned about blowing a tire — a common occurrence for the veteran ambulance driver.

When he neared a group of French soldiers who were marching on the badly scarred road, he laid on the horn. Sensing that the lives of comrades were in his care, they hustled off to the side, clearing the way for McConnell to roar past.

Screeching around one corner and then another, he almost lost control when the front left tire was punctured and went flat. *No, not now! We're so close!* He kept driving for two more blocks and then blew his horn as he pulled up to a large canvas tent emblazoned by a red cross. Within seconds, two *brancardiers* — stretcher bearers — burst out of the tent and, with McConnell's help, carted off the three soldiers one at a time.

The driver glanced at his watch. It had been thirty minutes from the moment he had picked up the casualties. Given the shelling and the pockmarked road, he was pleased — and even more so when the doctor later came out and told him, "I think they'll all survive."

That was McConnell's reward. He lived for days like this. It was the reason why the twenty-eight-year-old American had given up a well-paying job in North Carolina and was now risking his life in a foreign country to help save those fighting against the German invaders.

When war broke out in 1914, Americans who were living in Paris organized an *ambulance* — the French term for a temporary military hospital. Run by the American Hospital in Paris, the organization recruited volunteers to drive converted Model T cars into combat-torn areas and ferry the wounded and the dead. One of the drivers, A. Piatt Andrew, who was an official in former President William Howard Taft's administration, set up the American Ambulance Field Service (AAFS), which operated on the battlefields in northern France. The French government supplied the gasoline, oil, and tires, and housed and fed the volunteers.

The chassis of the Model T's were fitted with an ambulance body that accommodated three stretchers or six sitting wounded soldiers. The sturdy vehicles could drive off-road to let artillery and other convoys pass, cross fields, and run up steep and narrow bypaths to remote first-aid stations called *postes de secours*.

The ambulance drivers were all American volunteers, including budding authors such as eighteen-year-old Ernest Hemingway and poet e. e. Cummings. Nearly three hundred of the drivers were college-educated young men — half from Harvard, Princeton, and Yale — who mostly came from prominent families in the United States. McConnell was one of them.

In 1915, two years before America even had entered the war, he chose to risk life and limb for a cause that he and his fellow drivers had made their own. He didn't have to go. He wasn't drafted or pressured to join in this fight, because at the time the U.S. had taken a neutral position about the war. He could have continued living a life of relative ease.

Born into a wealthy Chicago family, James Rogers McConnell — Jim to his friends — attended private schools throughout his childhood. After his parents divorced, Jim spent several teenage years in France with his mother and two sisters, becoming fluent in French.

He then spent three years at the University of Virginia, where he planned to study law. A member of several campus organizations, Jim was editor-in-chief of the yearbook called *Corks and Curls*, assistant cheerleader, and president of the Aero Club, composed of students interested in the new field of aviation.

Although Jim excelled as a student, he was better known as a prank-loving fraternity boy with a great sense of humor. He was named "King of the Hot Feet" — he liked to sneak up on unsuspecting victims, pour lighter fluid on their shoes, and ignite them. He also enjoyed annoying his fellow students by donning full Scottish ceremonial clothes — including a kilt — and strolling around campus in the wee hours of the morning playing his bagpipe.

Jim withdrew from college — some say he was asked to leave — and worked in New York City before settling in Carthage, North Carolina, where he was an executive for a small railroad company as well as for the Carthage Board of Trade. He also wrote promotional pamphlets for the Sandhills region, a large pine tree–covered area that separates North Carolina's Piedmont region from the state's coastal plain.

The outbreak of war in Europe stirred McConnell's sense of adventure, so he made arrangements to become an ambulance driver. Days before leaving Carthage for France, he explained to a friend, "The war is the greatest event in history, and it's going on right now. I would be missing the opportunity of a lifetime if I don't experience it. The Sandhills will be here forever, but the war won't, and so I'm going. And I'll be of some use, too, not just as a sightseer looking on, because that wouldn't be fair."

He set sail from New York on the SS *Chicago* in early February of 1915 and crossed the Atlantic, which was teeming with enemy submarines. Fortunately, none attacked the ship. He arrived in France with one of the first groups of Americans to volunteer as drivers for the AAFS.

Thrust into duty amid gunfire and shelling, he transported the wounded from the Western Front to hospitals where doctors and nurses toiled nonstop. Those casualties that were considered hopeless were set aside to die in peace.

Like his comrades, McConnell was either on duty or on call twenty-four hours a day, seven days a week. During his breaks, he wrote articles for magazines about life as an ambulance driver.

"There are times following an attack when the drivers rest neither night nor day, when one gets food only in snatches," he wrote in a weekly called *The Outlook*. "Frequently, days at a time will pass when one is on such continuous service that there is never a chance to undress. Then there is the other aspect: the ever-present threat of being killed or wounded that one is under at the front because our section works and lives in a heavily shelled area."

Every day was more of the same for McConnell: transporting terribly wounded soldiers and hideously damaged bodies; seeing expressions of agony on the bloody faces of those alive and dead; driving past crumbled houses and through clouds of smoke and dust; hearing the frightening whistle of bombs and the screech of artillery shells as they hurtled down toward him; veering from murderous, ear-splitting explosions that flung their jagged shrapnel for a half mile in all directions, sometimes killing fellow ambulance drivers.

McConnell lived in a building in a town that was one of the most frequently bombarded places near the front. One day, the village was being shelled uncomfortably close to the ambulance headquarters, forcing McConnell and his comrades to take shelter in a cave that doubled as an ambulance repair shop. Just then, a call went out for an ambulance.

"I'll go," said McConnell.

"It's too dangerous right now," a fellow driver declared.

"It's always too dangerous," McConnell retorted as he hopped into his vehicle. Usually, he could time when the shells would fall, because the Germans tended to shoot their big guns in a certain pattern every three to five minutes. He would wait until the first ones struck before slipping out of the target area. But on this day, the shells were screaming into the village from different batteries. Rather than wait them out, he went anyway because lives were on the line.

While the town was being shelled, he sped down the streets, past the fresh rubble, and rambled to the *poste de secours* behind the trenches. As two casualties were being loaded into his ambulance, soldiers a few yards away shouted some gallows humor to McConnell: "Hey, driver, save a place for me tomorrow!" yelled one. Another chipped in, "When it's my turn, be sure to give me a quick ride!"

On the return trip, McConnell's ambulance was zooming down the main street of the village when a shell hit a house a half block away. He held his breath as he drove through the dust and debris that billowed from the blast. Emerging from the dirty haze, he took a deep breath and muttered, "Close, but I made it." Just then another shell exploded much nearer, the concussive force lifting the ambulance a few inches off the surface of the road. A hurtling piece of shrapnel slammed into the vehicle and sheared off part of the roof of the cabin on the driver's side only inches from McConnell's head. *That was much too close for comfort,* he thought.

After picking up the wounded at a dangerous *poste de secours* that was often in the line of fire, McConnell later was moved to write about the bleakness of one of the war's most fought-over sections: "It is a bit of land that before the war was covered with a magnificent forest. Now it is a wilderness whose desolation is beyond description. It is a section of murdered nature."

Working at night, especially when it was moonless, presented McConnell and his comrades a perilous hazard because they had to drive with their lights off. To keep them on would tip off the enemy of their location. So in the inky darkness, the drivers had to creep along, hoping that they would spot the fresh deep shell holes and fallen trees before it was too late. Many ambulances were damaged by these obstacles.

At night, McConnell would carefully drive past marching troops, horses, mule trains, baggage wagons, and ammunition carts. He would stop in front of armed sentinels who yelled, *"Halte là!"* After recognizing him, they would wave him on with an apologetic *"Passez."* The only time he went faster in the dark was when dazzling flares briefly lit up the area.

Besides the obvious dangers, the night brought the hardest work because that was when both sides tended to attack or counterattack. Of course, that meant more wounded and more dead. Sometimes all twenty of the unit's ambulances were pressed into service at once.

Early one morning McConnell answered an urgent call to pick up a gravely wounded soldier. The victim's comrades gathered around the ambulance to bid their friend good-bye. McConnell had seen enough casualties to know that life was slipping away for the soldier.

As the *brancardiers* placed the patient in the back of the vehicle, one of his buddies leaned over and told him, "See? You are going in an American car. You will have a good trip, old friend, so get well soon. Good-bye and good luck!"

His pals forced themselves to be positive and cheerful, but out of the soldier's earshot, their voices were low because they saw death creeping into his face. McConnell took his seat behind the wheel and started the engine.

"Wait!" shouted a soldier. "We need to get something for him."

Knowing time was of the essence, McConnell fumed, "Hurry! I need to get him to the hospital fast or he's a goner."

A half minute later, they returned and then he drove off. By the time the ambulance reached the hospital, McConnell discovered that the soldier was dead. *I should never have let those soldiers delay me from leaving. Why did they ask me to wait?* Then he noticed the ambulance was covered with sprigs of lilac and little yellow field flowers. *Now I understand.* The men knew the ambulance would serve as their comrade's hearse.

On the Fourth of July, the Americans in the ambulance service prepared for a big evening dinner party and had invited officers from all the regiments to attend the celebration. The headquarters was being decorated with flowers, and cooks were busy creating a scrumptious feast.

Unexpectedly, at 2 P.M., the earth began to tremble and the quiet afternoon was shattered by the thundering artillery explosions that barely drowned out the eruption of heavy machine gun and rifle fire. The Germans had launched a massive attack near Pont-à-Mousson. McConnell and the other drivers rushed to their vehicles, knowing there would be mounting casualties. They worked late into the night as the battle raged.

Arriving at a *poste de secours* within shouting distance of the enemy lines, McConnell ducked whizzing bullets as he helped load two soldiers who had been shot multiple times in the arms, legs, and torso. One of the soldiers struggled to get off the stretcher. "We can't leave without our lieutenant!" he yelled. "He's out there bleeding to death!"

"Where?" McConnell asked.

The soldier pointed toward the German trench and, while grimacing in pain, replied, "About one hundred yards away, near a barbed-wire barricade." A fading flare cast a greenish light on it. "You must go after him. Please, please! He's the one who carried me here after I was shot."

"Me too," said the other soldier. "After rescuing us, he went back out to retrieve the body of our commander. The lieutenant was dragging him when a flare lit up right over him, and the Germans saw him and gunned him down.

"We heard him shout that he'd been hit in the legs and couldn't move. I beg of you, bring him back."

McConnell took a deep breath and said, "All right. I'll try."

A *brancardier* gripped McConnell's arm to restrain him. "Are you crazy?" he whispered. "You'll be committing suicide if you go out there."

Pulling his arm away, McConnell replied, "What will be, will be." Then he crouched low and ran into the night. When another flare went off, he hit the ground and froze spread-eagled, hoping to avoid detection. Once the flare faded, he began low-crawling toward the barricade while bullets zipped inches above him. *I don't even know if he's alive,* McConnell thought. *And if he is, how am I going to get him back?*

Ever so slowly, he advanced to the barricade and found the French lieutenant sprawled by the barbed wire, groaning in pain. "Roll onto my back and put your arms around my neck," McConnell instructed. "I'm going to get you out of here."

"*Oui, oui, merci, merci* [Yes, yes, thank you, thank you]," murmured the officer, obviously weak from loss of blood.

With the lieutenant clinging to the American's neck, McConnell made the arduous crawl across the treacherous No Man's Land. Bullets kicked up dirt to his left and right, but none found their mark. Luckily, no flares were launched close enough for the two to be easily spotted by the enemy. For what seemed to take hours, but took about twenty hard minutes, McConnell brought the lieutenant to the ambulance.

Drenched in sweat and mud, McConnell slipped behind the steering wheel and let out a long exhale. *Well,* he thought, *I asked for adventure.*

His night was far from over. He made several more trips to transport casualties and didn't get to bed until 3:30 ' -L - By then, he and his comrades had carried more than three hundred and fifty wounded soldiers to the hospital.

The next morning, over coffee, Leslie Buswell, a fellow driver and close friend, congratulated McConnell on his courageous rescue. McConnell modestly brushed it off, saying, "I'm grateful things worked out. It's a tough business out there."

"Jim, the horror of this war is growing on me day by day," Buswell confessed. "Sometimes when I'm trying to get a few hours' sleep on a stretcher, the blood, the broken arms, and the mutilated trunks haunt me, and I feel I can hardly go through another day of it."

"The misery gets to me, too," McConnell admitted.

"But here's the miracle," Buswell added. "All of that is

soon forgotten when a call comes, and you see those ban-daged soldiers waiting to be taken to a hospital."

Being so far from America for so long, McConnell and his fellow drivers relished receiving letters and packages from home. They were eager for any news from their own towns, so they cherished newspapers and magazines, which they read cover to cover before passing them on. When all the drivers had finished reading the periodicals, they would drop them off at the trenches so the soldiers could enjoy them, too.

In an article for *The Outlook*, McConnell wrote, "The men from the trenches are surprised that we have volun-tarily undertaken such a hazardous occupation, and express their appreciation and gratitude with almost embarrassing frequency. 'You render a great service,' say the officers, and those of highest rank call to render thanks in the name of France. It is good to feel that one's endeavors are appreci-ated, and it's encouraging to hear the words of praise.

"But then there are times when at the end of an evacua-tion, one draws a stretcher from the car and the poor wounded man, who has never groaned during a ride that must have been painful, holds out his hand, grasps yours, and, forcing a smile, murmurs, '*Merci.*' That is what urges you to hurry back for other wounded, to be glad that there is a risk to one's self in helping them, and to feel grateful that you have the opportunity to serve the brave French people in their sublime struggle."

*   *   *

Ernest Hemingway used his own experiences as an ambulance driver to form the basis of his classic novel, A Farewell to Arms.

After the United States entered the war on April 6, 1917, the American Ambulance Field Service was eventually merged into the U.S. Army. While serving as drivers with AAFS, 151 men were killed, including 21 Harvard students. During the war, about 2,500 young men served at various times as ambulance drivers.

For risking his life to rescue the lieutenant, the French government awarded McConnell the Croix de Guerre, one of that country's highest military awards for "courage and fearlessness worthy of the highest praise."

But being an ambulance driver was not enough for him. He later wrote in his book Flying for France, "The more I saw the splendor of the fight the French were fighting, the more I began to feel like [a slacker]. So I made up my mind to go into aviation."

He earned his wings in 1916 and became one of the original pilots of the famed Lafayette Escadrille, a volunteer American air squadron that fought for France. He sustained injuries in several crashes and was credited with four victories.

On March 13, 1917, the day before his thirtieth birthday, McConnell wrote in his diary, "This war may kill me, but I have it to thank for much."

Six days later, he was shot down and killed during a dogfight with two German planes above the Somme battlefields, near the village of Flavy-le-Martel, Aisne. He was the last American pilot to die under French colors before the United States formally entered the war a month later.

His fellow pilots honored his wish to be buried where he fell in battle, which was in an apple orchard. French soldiers used stones from a nearby ruined building to build a monument to him. A villager and her daughter maintained the grave, which peasants in the area considered a shrine. "It will always be covered with flowers," the daughter said at the time. "You know, he was a volunteer."

In 1928, McConnell's body was exhumed. Along with the bodies of eight other fallen comrades of the Escadrille, he was reburied in a crypt at the Lafayette Memorial in Marnes-la-Coquette near Paris.

McConnell is memorialized with a statue called The Aviator at the University of Virginia that bears the inscription: "Soaring like an eagle into new heavens of valor and devotion." The base of a monument erected in his hometown of Carthage, North Carolina, says, in part, "He fought for Humanity, Liberty and Democracy, lighted the way for his countrymen and showed all men how to dare nobly and to die gloriously."

THE KILLER MARKSMAN

Army Lieutenant Samuel Woodfill

I'm trapped and I can't do a thing!

Lieutenant Samuel Woodfill lay flat on his stomach in a shallow depression at the bottom of a ravine, unable to even shoot back because the Germans were sweeping the area with deadly machine gun fire just inches above the ground. The depression wasn't deep enough to protect his stuffed backpack, and he felt it getting riddled with bullet holes.

Moments earlier he had been leading his platoon down a slope in France's Argonne Forest when his outfit met deadly resistance.

Above the intense *rat-a-tat-tat* of the enemy machine guns, Woodfill heard a different, more terrifying sound — the whine of a German artillery shell. It grew increasingly louder until it exploded in a brain-jarring blast only a few yards away from him. Then a second one landed even closer, showering him with dirt and rocks.

The jig is up, thought the veteran officer. *Maybe the next one has my name on it.* He didn't want to die without scribbling a final message to his beloved wife, Lorena. Having always kept a wedding day picture of her in his shirt pocket, he pulled it out and fumbled around his pants for a pencil. On the back of the photo, he wrote Lorena's address in Fort Thomas, Kentucky.

As bullets zipped mere inches above his head and exploding shells thundered all around him, Woodfill scribbled what he was sure would be his farewell message:

"October 11, 1918

"In case of accident or Death, it is my last and fondest desire that the finder of my remains shall please do me a last, and everlasting, favor to please forward this picture to my Darling Wife. And tell her that I have fallen on the field of honor, and departed to a better land which knows no sorrow and feels no pain. I will prepare a place and be waiting at the Golden Gate of Heaven for the arrival of my Darling Blossom."

Woodfill, a professional soldier for seventeen years, had been in trouble spots throughout the world. But he had never experienced anything as intense as this.

Growing up in southern Indiana where he quit school after the fourth grade, Woodfill was a tall, strapping eighteen-year-old when he joined the army in 1901. He battled guerrillas in the Philippines, served in Alaska, and fought bandits on the Mexican border.

Now here he was in the midst of an ongoing, bloody battle that was lasting weeks in a sector bordered on the east by the Meuse River and on the west by the dense Argonne Forest. As a lieutenant in Company M, 60th Infantry Regiment, 5th Division, he was in charge of a platoon of mostly inexperienced and untested recruits and draftees.

They were all part of a massive offensive by the American First Army, commanded by General John "Black Jack" Pershing and French forces. The army's objective was to break through the German defenses for more than thirty miles to a critical railway junction near Sedan, France. Because its capture would inflict a knockout punch to the flow of supplies to the German military, enemy forces were under orders to stop the Americans at all costs.

Days before Woodfill's men had experienced the enemy's wrath, they were marching toward the front, itching to "get in the fight." During a break when they stopped to eat lunch, Woodfill warned them that German troops were only a few miles ahead. As the troops gathered in the chow line, he told them to enjoy their hot meal because it might be a long time before they get one again.

"Make it snappy, you guys," a mess sergeant growled at the rookie doughboys as he dished out the grub. "This ain't no all-night barbecue. And if you birds want to get in on the buffet supper, you'd better hop to it while the goin's good.

Those Germans up ahead are liable to ruin your appetite any minute."

Seconds later, a German artillery shell screeched overhead and slammed to the ground nearby in a thunderous roar. Mess kits flew in all directions. Eight young privates scrambled under the table where the cook had been ladling out the food. In their haste, they knocked over the table, spilling pots of stew, fried potatoes, and coffee all over themselves.

Woodfill, who watched the scene unfold while sitting against a tree, just shook his head. Although he was quite uneasy about the bombardment — especially when another shell landed even closer — the thirty-five-year-old lieutenant figured the Germans weren't trying to target his outfit but rather the French artillery nearby.

Noticing that two fellow lieutenants were waiting to see how he would react, he told himself, *It's up to me to appear calm, otherwise some might panic.* So he took another spoonful of stew, although it stuck in his throat because he was getting more alarmed by the minute. He just couldn't show it.

Another shell exploded on a road about fifty yards away and maimed several members of a French crew that was moving a horse-drawn artillery gun. Scared by the blast, the horses bolted, sending the big gun rolling end over end down an embankment.

Seeing that the survivors of the crew needed help, Woodfill jumped up and shouted to his men, "Who will volunteer to help me haul that gun back up the embankment?"

Several men — mostly veterans because the newcomers were still cowering in various shelters trying to protect themselves from the shelling — stepped forward.

"The sooner we assist the Frenchies to get on down the road and out of our neighborhood, the sooner the Germans will allow us to finish our first hot meal near the front, without seasoning our stew with any more lead and steel," Woodfill told them.

Grabbing ropes, the Americans hustled to the embankment, turned the gun right side up, and began lugging it up. The shelling grew worse.

Hearing another terrifying whistling overhead, Woodfill could tell from the sound that this one would find its mark right where he was standing. He dived to the ground and hoped death would be quick. Curling up in a ball, he closed his eyes for what he felt sure would be the last time ever. The shell tore through the branches of a tree above him and landed just a few feet away, right between him and a French artilleryman. He felt the impact, but, miraculously, the shell didn't explode. *It's a dud!* he thought, still so tense that his muscles refused to relax.

Staring at the half-buried shell, the Frenchman exclaimed, "*Mon Dieu* [My God]*!*"

In response, Woodfill shook his head in amazement, too stunned to speak. Once he processed how incredibly lucky he was, he completed the task of helping haul the French gun back up and onto the road. Then he returned to his lunch spot and finished the meal that had been so rudely interrupted.

Woodfill was determined to set a good example for the rookies. He knew they were bound to make mistakes, possibly with disastrous results. But he also knew they weren't afraid to fight.

One night, after they settled down in trenches that the French had dug for earlier battles, Woodfill deployed sentries to various sectors around the perimeter.

At about 3 A.M., he was jolted awake by the sound of grenade blasts coming from one particular trench. Thinking they were being attacked, he grabbed his weapon and charged over to the spot, which was now strangely quiet. The sentry on duty was lying unconscious at the bottom of the trench. There was no sign of the enemy.

After the sentry, a baby-faced rookie, was revived and questioned, Woodfill pieced together what had happened: The skittish young soldier thought he heard some suspicious sounds out in front, so he threw a hand grenade from the trench. But he forgot that the French had strung up wire netting along the top of the trench as a protective barrier against the enemy. In the dark, he couldn't see the netting. The grenade hit the wire and bounced right back over his head to the rear of the trench and went off behind him.

Believing the enemy had tossed back the grenade, he shouted, "Come on, you lousy Germans! I can lick your whole army!" Then he began hurling one grenade after another —

all of which rebounded off the netting and exploded near him in what he was convinced was a full-scale enemy assault. The only thing that saved him from wasting a whole stack of grenades was that one of them exploded so close to him that it had knocked him out. *That's one crazy rookie mistake,* Woodfill thought.

A few days later, Woodfill was ordered to have four members of his platoon repair some barbed-wire entanglements that were damaged during a German attack. *This isn't a job for butterfingered rookies,* he thought. Deciding to lead the detail himself, he picked three men who were experienced soldiers. Reaching the seventy-foot-wide-by-six-foot-tall barbed-wire barricade, Woodfill lay on his stomach and weaved new wire to close the gap while the others covered him and scanned the area for snipers.

With another spool of wire, he crawled over the crest of a hill for further repairs, when a bullet flew past his ear like the crack of a whip. Then machine gun fire erupted, kicking up dirt and rocks within two feet of him. Even though he was already on his stomach, he tried to flatten himself in the ground. He remained completely motionless and barely breathed for several minutes until the shooting stopped. *The gunner must think I'm dead,* he thought.

Ever so slowly he slithered backward to his men and said, "Those Germans don't seem to like me."

One of the soldiers cracked, "What did you expect 'em to do? Serve you beer?"

A few days later, on October 11, 1918, Woodfill and his platoon trekked toward the front, passing burned-out villages, water-filled shell craters, and stripped-bare woods of the Meuse-Argonne region. The conditions were miserable — thick mud, howling winds, and icy rain — for the men who were dead-tired from being constantly on the move in an Allied effort to push back the German advance.

Woodfill was worried because his outfit of newbies was going against the world's best-trained army. The enemy controlled hilltops, forests, and ridges where machine gun fire and artillery had been unleashing death and destruction for days. This day was no different.

Forced to crouch or crawl, Woodfill led his men down the slope of an open ravine. A murderous round of bullets tore into the doughboys. Reaching the bottom of the ravine, Woodfill and the surviving members of his platoon found cover wherever they could.

He lunged into a shallow depression near some partially buried scraps of corrugated iron. Then the shelling started. That's when he feared, *Maybe the next one has my name on it*, and wrote the farewell note to his wife on the back of her photo.

Soon the enemy ceased shooting and shelling. Cautiously emerging from the depression that had given him the barest of protection, Woodfill took a deep breath and thought, *I guessed wrong. There is no German ammunition with my name on it — at least not today.*

He and his platoon hiked out of the ravine and past the ruins of Madeleine Farm, where they halted behind the crest of a ridge. Drenched in sheets of freezing rain, they plopped into shell craters and shivered. At nightfall, Woodfill took eight men to scout the woods beyond the ridge. On the way back, he stepped onto a small bridge that the Germans had booby-trapped. Inadvertently tripping a hidden wire, he triggered a small explosive that had been planted in a nearby tree directly above him. The blast knocked him out.

When he regained consciousness, blood was pouring from his nose, and his head hurt, but he seemed otherwise uninjured. Staggering back to the rest of his unit, Woodfill collapsed in a funk hole and fell asleep. A few hours later, he woke up and found himself floating out of the hole because it was overflowing from the pouring rain.

At dawn the rain had stopped, and a dense fog shrouded the area. Woodfill was ordered to lead a reconnaissance mission into the woods and pinpoint the location of the German lines. With bayonets fixed and rifles ready, the cold, mud-caked soldiers moved out.

The fog provided an excellent cover for the Americans until they entered another ravine. Within minutes the fog lifted, revealing their presence to the enemy, which immediately opened up with trench mortars and machine guns. Caught out in the open, the doughboys fled in all directions in search of cover. A sergeant running next to Woodfill toppled over dead. Ahead of him, soldiers were being blown off their feet by mortar rounds. But most of the casualties were coming from enemy machine guns.

I have to find those guns and take them out, Woodfill told himself. Motioning his men to stay back, Woodfill dumped his pack and worked his way across a 150-yard-wide field by crawling from shell hole to shell hole. Bullets passed so close to his face that he could feel their heat. He scampered to a dirt road and then crawled in a ditch, where he spotted three separate machine gun emplacements — a church bell tower in the village of Cunel about three hundred yards to his left, the loft of an old stable about half that distance to his right, and a hidden nest in the woods straight ahead. He couldn't see any of the gunners, only their muzzle flashes.

Few, if any, soldiers in the battalion were a better marksman than Woodfill. From the time he was old enough to pull the trigger, he had been hunting with the musket his father had carried in the Mexican-American War and Civil War. By age ten, the boy was considered a superior shot. As he grew up, he became an expert rifleman, once shooting three caribou in Alaska from nearly a mile away. He could hold his weapon as steady as if it were resting on a tripod.

Now his shooting skill was being put to the ultimate test. From his muddy position in the ditch, he slid his rifle forward and placed the butt against his shoulder without exposing any part of his body. He studied the muzzle flash of the machine gun in the church tower, then moved his point of aim to where he figured the gunner's head would be and fired, killing him. Woodfill waited until the next person on the gun crew took the slain man's place and shot him, too. It took Woodfill only five bullets to kill all five members of that crew.

Despite a steady bombardment of artillery, a thin mist, and clouds of battlefield smoke and dust, he steadied his aim at the stable loft and fired into a gap in the boards, silencing that machine gun, too.

Fearing that his position had been compromised, he bolted for a new location as bullets nipped at his heels. He rolled into a shell hole and within seconds was struggling to breathe. His eyes, nose, and throat felt as if they were on fire. *Gas!* A trace of deadly mustard gas that the enemy had deployed earlier still lingered in the crater and was now attacking him. A strong dose of the poison gas could burn a victim's lungs, blind him, and burn his skin. *I have to get out of here! Where to go, where to go?* Looking through his blurry, pain-racked eyes, he frantically scanned the area for better cover. His only option was a patch of thistles several yards away.

Still gasping for breath, he dashed out of the crater and, dodging bullets, leaped into the thicket. He crawled behind it to an open space and gulped fresh air. Like many of his comrades, Woodfill seldom used his gas mask because it limited his scope of vision.

Ignoring the agony from the effects of the gas, he crawled to an old gravel pile where he had a good angle on the third machine gun nest not far away. He took out his automatic pistol and a clip for his rifle. Then he pushed the barrel of

his rifle slowly over the top of the gravel pile
through the sights. Tears caused by the gas still fl
stinging eyes, so it was hard for him to see. Blinkin
stantly, he caught the outline of an enemy helmet and fi   i.
Down went the soldier, but another took his place. Woodfill
fired again. That German died, too. One by one, Woodfill took
out four members of the gun crew. Two more Germans
tried to flee. Woodfill used the last bullet in his clip to drop
the first one and then calmly picked up his .45 pistol and
shot the second one.

By now the woods reverberated with the din of nonstop
machine gun fire from both sides, accompanied by trench
mortars and artillery. Still in pain and finding it difficult to
see clearly without blinking, he sprinted toward an area
where he thought he might find his platoon. He approached
what appeared to be a large dead German lying in the mud.
But as Woodfill ran by him, the German leaped to his feet,
grabbed the rifle of the startled American, and threw it into
the brush. While the German fumbled to get a Luger out of
his holster, Woodfill beat him to the draw and killed him.

After finding his rifle, Woodfill ran until he came across
a German machine gun nest that had been sweeping the
woods with fire. As he had done before, he took out this
five-man gun crew one at a time.

Farther ahead, he spotted yet another machine gun nest.
He dropped to his stomach and low-crawled through the
mud until he got into position. Then he wiped out that five-
man enemy team with lethally placed shots.

Coming under new fire from his right, Woodfill sought refuge in an enemy trench that he hoped was abandoned. It wasn't. When he dived into the trench, he landed on top of a surprised German officer who was armed with a Luger. Both were momentarily shocked by the other, but Woodfill reacted quicker with his pistol and shot him.

Seconds later, another German confronted him. Woodfill's pistol jammed, so he grabbed a pickax that was in easy reach and swung it at the soldier just as the foe was raising his rifle. Whacked in the head, the German went down in a heap.

A bullet then nearly missed Woodfill, who whirled around and saw that the officer he had shot was still alive and had just fired his Luger. Woodfill finished him off with the pickax.

The sharpshooting, tough lieutenant had single-handedly taken out all the enemy machine guns in that sector, allowing his battalion to move deeper into the forest. His remarkable feat helped pave the way for the Allied forces to ultimately win the battle that was instrumental in ending the war.

Samuel Woodfill was evacuated and treated for severe effects of mustard gas and wasn't fit for duty until after Germany surrendered. He suffered lung problems the rest of his life.

On February 19, 1919, General John Pershing presented Woodfill with the Medal of Honor and promoted him to captain, declaring that the hero was "America's greatest doughboy." Receiving medals from six countries, Woodfill became the army's most decorated soldier of World War I.

After Woodfill returned to civilian life, he suffered financial difficulties when his orchard business in Indiana failed. He took on low-paying jobs as a watchman at a mill and as a carpenter, but could barely support himself and his wife on his skimpy salary and meager military pension.

When World War II broke out in 1942, the army gave him a commission as a major and assigned him the role of a rifle instructor in Alabama. Widowed two years later, he eventually retired to Vevay, Indiana, where he died in 1951 at the age of sixty-eight — broke and alone. He was laid to rest in a local cemetery. But through the efforts of citizens who appreciated his service to his country, his body was moved to Arlington National Cemetery, where he was buried with full military honors thirty yards from the grave of his commanding officer, General Pershing.

THE ACE OF ACES
United States Air Service
Captain Eddie Rickenbacker

C aptain Eddie Rickenbacker sat down on his bunk, pulled out his diary, and wrote, "Sept. 24, 1918 — Just been promoted to command of 94th Aero Squadron. I shall never ask a pilot to go on any mission I won't go on."

The next morning — his first full day as commander — America's top ace took off alone at daybreak and flew near the French town of Verdun, looking for enemy planes. It didn't take long until he found them — a pair of two-man reconnaissance aircraft known as LVGs that were being escorted by five single-pilot fighter planes called Fokkers.

Rickenbacker climbed toward the sun and escaped detection, circling well to their rear. But he didn't hide for long. Despite being outnumbered seven to one, the gutsy pilot chose to attack. He shut down his engine so he could silently sneak up from behind, went into a dive, and made a beeline for the trailing Fokker.

By the time the German pilot realized he was targeted, it was too late for him to escape. Rickenbacker had him in his sights and fired both his guns for a long burst. The German tried to pull away, but the bullets were already ripping through his fuselage, killing him instantly. Trailing black smoke, his plane plunged to the ground.

Rickenbacker had planned to zoom up to protect himself from retaliation from the four remaining Fokkers. But then he noticed that his surprise attack had shaken the pilots so badly that they veered off to save their own skins, allowing him to dive through their formation and go after the two LVGs.

The pilots in both those planes had witnessed his attack and tried to shake off Rickenbacker by diving while the airmen in the rear seats were firing their machine guns at him. The ace glanced over his shoulder and saw that the four Fokkers had not yet gathered in an attack formation. *I still have a few seconds before they come after me,* he thought.

He swooped under the nearest LVG and was about to shoot at its belly when the crafty German pilot banked sharply, giving the gunner good aim at Rickenbacker who was forced to delay shooting until he got into a better position. Just then he saw tracer bullets streaking past his head. The other LVG had come up behind him so that Rickenbacker was now the prey. He immediately zoomed up and momentarily out of range.

For the next minute, the three planes dodged and weaved in the dogfight while the four Fokkers were still regaining their formation. The wind currents had pushed the planes farther into Germany. *I'm running low on fuel,* he thought. *I'll try one more attack, and if it fails, I'll try to hightail it back to my own lines before it's too late.*

He drew to within fifty yards of the closest LVG. Ignoring the enemy bullets, he leveled his plane and kept firing until the LVG burst into flames. It flipped over and over until it crashed. Meanwhile, the four Fokkers and the other LVG went after him with a vengeance. But after a couple of nifty maneuvers, he gave his plane full throttle and escaped from the slower German aircraft.

As he crossed into friendly territory, Rickenbacker allowed himself to gloat. As pleased as he was about notching two more victories, he was even more satisfied that he had proven to the men in his squadron that he would indeed lead by example.

It came as no surprise to anyone who knew Eddie Rickenbacker in his younger days that he was destined for greatness, even though he dropped out of school at age thirteen. He did it to help support his family following the unexpected death of his father. Fascinated by machines, Eddie took correspondence courses in auto mechanics and eventually worked at a repair shop, an auto factory, and a car dealership. In his twenties, he became a professional race car driver who competed in the Indianapolis 500 four times and set a record for speed at 134 miles per hour. Nicknamed "Fast Eddie," he was earning more than $40,000 a year — a huge sum back then.

When the United States entered World War I in 1917, he tried to convince the military to hire race car drivers as pilots because such men were used to high speeds and confined spaces. But his idea was rejected. Undaunted, he enlisted in the Army and, as a sergeant first class, was sent to an aviation training facility in France. While serving as an engineering officer and teaching mechanics, he learned to fly in his spare time.

Eventually, he was assigned to the 94th Aero Squadron, the first flying unit sent to the front under the banner of the United States Air Service (forerunner of the U.S. Air Force). Based at an aerodrome in Toul, France, Rickenbacker and the other pilots called themselves the "Hat in the Ring" squad. They sported an insignia that featured Uncle Sam's red-white-and-blue top hat and a stars-and-stripes hatband. The circle around the hat represented an old custom of throwing one's hat into a ring as a call to battle.

Although "Rick," as he was known by his comrades, had a daredevil reputation, he was no different than the other inexperienced pilots in the squadron when it came to wondering about his fate. He accepted the danger. But always lurking in the back of his mind was the thought that luck could desert him in an instant and spell his doom.

The Americans were given Nieuport 28s to fly — a biplane that the British and French aviators had discarded or wouldn't fly because it was considered so inferior. Although it was fast and maneuverable, its wings were fragile, its engine unreliable, and its machine guns temperamental. And while many pilots from the other countries, including Germany, had parachutes, the Americans weren't given any.

On April 14, 1918, the squadron flew the first official combat patrol for the United States — and shot down two enemy planes. Two weeks later, on April 29, Rickenbacker scored his first victory, blasting a German fighter plane called a Pfalz out of the sky. With each passing day, he grew more confident, and as doubts about his flying ability diminished, disdain for his foes increased.

On May 17, Rickenbacker was cruising behind enemy lines at eighteen thousand feet, looking for a German plane to shoot down. His patience paid off when he spotted three aircraft known as Albatroses flying below him in a spread-out formation.

With his eyes locked on the trailing plane, Rick shoved his stick forward and dived. Pushing his Nieuport to two hundred miles per hour — way past its maximum speed — he kept its nose pointing at the tail of an Albatros, which was now darting steeply downward to escape him. *He's trying to outdive me instead of outmaneuver me,* Rickenbacker thought. *What a blunder.* As the distance closed to within fifty yards, Rick began shooting and saw his flaming bullets pierce the back of the pilot's seat. Seconds later, the plane began to flutter and then fall.

While still in a steep dive and following his stricken foe, Rickenbacker was aware that he himself was in a vulnerable spot because the other two planes were on his tail. All alone, he knew he needed to rely on his own maneuvers to escape them. He pulled the joystick back and began a sharp climb. That's when he heard a loud *crack* and a sickening ripping sound. The strain on the plane going from a dive to a climb had collapsed his top right wing, sheering off the entire spread of canvas. Without any supporting surface on the wing, the Nieuport turned over on its right side. The nose was forced down and, despite his efforts with the joystick and rudder, the plane went into a tight spin. All the while the other two Albatroses followed him, firing bullets into his crippled craft during his seemingly fatal plunge.

For a pilot who appeared doomed to crash, Rickenbacker wasn't thinking of himself. *Why are they wasting ammunition?* he thought. *How stupid they must be to believe I'm faking this so they'll leave me alone. They're fools not to know when an airplane is actually about to crash. The whole spread of the wing's fabric is gone. No pilot can fly without fabric on his machine.*

Where will I crash? There are woods below me. Heavens! How much nearer the ground is getting! Will the whole framework of my machine disintegrate and fling me out to the mercy of the four winds? Maybe if I strike the treetops, it's barely possible that I might escape with a score of broken bones. Never will I fly a Nieuport again if I get out of this fix alive! But no use worrying about that now. Either I'll die or be a mangled prisoner in Germany. Which would Mother rather have?

The image of his mother opening a telegram telling her that he was dead roused his fighting spirit. He kept fighting the controls but could do nothing to stop the tailspin. Having fallen ten thousand feet since the wing collapsed, he looked down and figured he was now only three thousand feet from crashing. He could see Germans standing on the road gazing up at him. *They're already celebrating over the souvenirs they'll get from my machine — and from my body.*

There was one thing he could try — open the throttle all the way. It would either hasten his death or possibly prevent it. He pulled it open and gained even greater speed . . . and suddenly the tailspin stopped and the plane leveled out. Regaining control of the Nieuport, he thought, *If only I can keep her airborne for five minutes, I might make our lines.* He looked above and below. *Good. No planes in the sky.* His pursuers had broken off contact with him, convinced he would crash. Flying low because the damaged plane wouldn't climb, Rickenbacker encountered enemy antiaircraft fire. But he was so relieved he hadn't slammed into the ground that he ignored bursting shells around him.

The plane was losing altitude as it crossed into friendly territory. Minutes later, with the engine still running wide open, the Nieuport grazed the top of the squadron's hangar and pancaked onto the aerodrome's field. He walked away without a scratch.

Early the next day, the French notified Rickenbacker that they had witnessed his latest victory. The German pilot he had killed had fallen on the controls in such a way that the Albatros had flown toward France and landed a few hundred yards inside the French line. It was Rick's second confirmed kill.

The American pilots were overwhelmingly outnumbered, poorly supported, and woefully equipped, both in machines and experience. The losses during July were dreadful — thirty-six pilots were either captured or killed. Among those who died was Quentin Roosevelt, the twenty-year-old son of former President Teddy Roosevelt, who fell in flames on July 14, 1918. The Americans, however, had scored thirty-eight victories during the same period.

Rickenbacker's squadron finally received better aircraft, known as SPADs — fast, maneuverable biplanes that could climb higher and survive faster dives and turns than the old Nieuports.

While leading a patrol over enemy territory, Rick encountered a dogfight in progress between the French and Germans. Seeing a French SPAD in trouble, Rickenbacker went to his aid without checking to see where all the enemy planes were located. A German Fokker was closing in on the SPAD when Rickenbacker came up on the enemy's tail and fired a short burst. The Fokker turned over and fell earthward out of control.

Before he could exult in another victory, Rickenbacker was badly scared a moment later by seeing flaming bullets streak past his head. He immediately threw his plane into a tailspin to get out of the line of fire and then raced home. *Never again will I venture into hostile skies without twisting my neck in all directions every moment of the flight!* he promised himself.

One by one, the American ace with the most victories was shot down. First there was Major Raoul Lufbery, who was killed, then Paul Baer (who survived and was taken prisoner), followed by the deaths of David Putnam and Frank Luke. Now Rickenbacker found himself as the new American Ace of Aces. Although he was proud of being the No. 1 ace, he was haunted by a superstition that the title would bring the same unavoidable death that befell its previous title holders. "I want it [the title] and yet I fear it," he confided to a fellow airman. "I feel that this superstition is almost the heaviest burden that I carry with me in the air. Perhaps it serves to redouble my caution and sharpen my fighting senses. But I can't forget that the life of a titleholder is short."

On September 24, Rickenbacker was named the new commander of the 94th Aero Squadron.

Addressing his men for the first time as their leader, he told them, "I want no saluting, no unnecessary deference to rank. What I want are victories. We're all in this together, pilots and mechanics. We need each other and we're going to work together as equals, each man doing his job." He told them he would lead by example from the cockpit, not from a desk. It was the next morning when he shot down those two enemy planes — the first time he had ever scored twin victories in one day.

Two days later, while flying over enemy territory right before daybreak, he encountered a German Fokker that was heading straight toward him. Both he and the enemy pilot began firing directly at each other at the same time as they flew closer and closer. *Are we going to collide, or will he get out of the way?* Rickenbacker wondered.

The German dived under him, so Rick instantly made a loop that put him behind the enemy's tail. Training his sights on the center of the enemy fuselage, the ace pulled the trigger on both his machine guns. With one long burst, the fight was over and the Fokker crumpled to the ground.

The joy from his latest victory was quickly replaced by concern, because his engine developed a violent vibration. He had recurring visions of crashing in Germany and ending up a POW. Throttling down to reduce the pounding, he was able to maintain headway. *If my motor fails completely, I'm doomed,* he thought. At less than a thousand feet altitude, he knew he could glide only a few hundred yards if the engine conked out. Fortunately, he made it to an aerodrome in Verdun. When he examined the plane, he discovered that one blade of his propeller had been shot off by his foe during their head-on attack.

Early the next morning, he spotted a huge enemy observation balloon about twenty miles inside Germany. It was attached to a cable fastened to a truck that was towing it toward the front. *This is just the target I've been searching for!* Rick told himself. He blasted away until he was so close he had to climb straight up to avoid crashing into it. Just as his SPAD's nose pointed skyward, he heard the *rat-tat-tat* of a machine gun from the truck below him. One of the bullets struck his seat, right next to his ear. Another severed a wire in the tail.

As he banked the plane, he looked behind and saw the interior of the balloon ignite and then burst into bright flames. He had just recorded his eleventh victory. Carefully, he brought his SPAD back to Verdun for another inspection. A neat row of bullet holes ran back down from the tail toward the cockpit. The last hole was only four inches from the pad on which he rested his head. "The gunners on the truck had done an excellent bit of shooting," Rickenbacker told the mechanic.

"Is dropping in on me going to be a daily occurrence?" the mechanic asked. "Yesterday it was a broken prop and today a broken tail."

On the afternoon of October 10, the 94th Aero Squadron received orders to destroy two bothersome enemy observation balloons in German-occupied territory. Rick and thirteen of his aviators were joined by eight planes from the 147th and seven from the 27th Squadrons. Before they reached the target area, they were met by about two dozen enemy planes, including some from the infamous Red Baron's Flying Circus — the name given to German ace

Manfred von Richthofen's squadron. The encounter turned into two huge dogfights involving two dozen aircraft in different areas of the sky.

Within minutes, Rickenbacker bore down on the tail of an enemy Fokker and fired a burst that struck the fuel tank. As the burning plane spun in a death spiral, Rick saw the pilot jump out and open his parachute. *Why,* the ace wondered, *do the Germans have all these humane devices and our own country couldn't at least copy them to save American pilots from being burned to a crisp?*

He noticed that a rookie pilot from the 147th was in serious trouble because a Fokker was right on his tail. Suddenly, Lieutenant Wilburt White, that squadron's beloved leader and an ace, tried to save him from certain death. Swooping in from the front, White flew directly toward the Fokker until both planes were streaking at each other at more than one hundred miles per hour. Without firing a shot, White rammed the Fokker head-on. The two planes telescoped into each other in a violent impact as wings went through wings. Fragments twirled in all directions before the crumpled fuselages fell swiftly and landed in one heap on the banks of the Meuse River. The horrendous crash caused the Germans to give up the dogfight and fly off.

Even though Rickenbacker was shaken by what he had just witnessed, he flew over to the other dogfight involving Germans and the 27th and 147th Aero Squadrons. He saw a SPAD passing by him with two Fokkers on his comrade's tail, filling the fuselage with tracer bullets. He recognized the SPAD pilot as his friend Jimmy Meissner. Rick quickly turned until he was lined up with the rear enemy plane and let go with a long burst from his machine guns. The Fokker went out of control and smashed into the ground for the ace's nineteenth kill. Moments later, the other Fokker fled.

It was the third time that Rickenbacker had come along in the nick of time to get Meissner out of trouble. Twice before on the old Nieuports, Meissner had torn off his wings in too sudden of a maneuver and was wobbling home when he was attacked, only to be saved when Rickenbacker arrived on the scene to shoot down each foe.

Back at the aerodrome, Rick and his fellow aviators grieved over White's death. "For sheer nerve and bravery I believe this heroic feat will never be surpassed," Rickenbacker told his men. "No national honor is too great to compensate his family for this sacrifice for his comrade pilot." Adding to the heartache, it was White's last scheduled mission before going on leave to visit his wife and two small children in Connecticut.

As the war entered its final days, Eddie Rickenbacker had logged more hours in the air than any other pilot in the United States Air Service. He fought in 134 air battles and shot down 26 enemy planes, giving him the title of America's Ace of Aces and earning the Distinguished Service Cross nine times. During those harrowing months of combat, he survived engine failures, shredded wings, antiaircraft fire, and thousands of enemy bullets. Time and again he returned to the aerodrome in a plane so full of holes from bullets and shrapnel that mechanics were amazed it flew. He volunteered for dozens of one-man missions over German-occupied territory and often single-handedly engaged enemy planes even when he was outnumbered. Incredibly, not once was he even slightly wounded.

On the morning of November 11 — shortly before the war's official cease-fire — Rickenbacker was flying low over No Man's Land, gazing below at German and American infantrymen huddled in their funk holes and trenches. A few Germans took some potshots at him.

But then at the moment of the cease-fire, he witnessed an incredible sight. From overhead, he watched the soldiers from both sides throw their helmets in the air, toss their guns aside, and wave to one another. Then all up and down the front, Germans and Americans, who just minutes earlier were willing to shoot each other, were now cautiously edging forward to meet. Continuing to circle over them, Rick watched them embracing, dancing, and cheering. Some were even kissing each other on both cheeks.

Rickenbacker smiled and thought, *The war really is over.*

Shortly after the war, Rickenbacker wrote an account of his war days called Fighting the Flying Circus, *which provided much of the material for this story. Hailed as a hero, he went on a lecture tour. In 1920 he founded the Rickenbacker Automobile Company and developed the first car with both front and rear brakes. But the company went bankrupt in 1927, putting him deep in debt. "Here in America failure is* not the end of the world," he said at the time. "If you have the determination, you can come back from failure and succeed."

And he did. He bought the Indianapolis Motor Speedway and turned it into a success with its famed Memorial Day 500. He then invested in other businesses.

In 1930 — twelve years after the war — President Herbert Hoover belatedly presented Rickenbacker with the Medal of Honor for single-handedly attacking a German patrol when he was outnumbered seven to one.

Eventually, Rickenbacker and several investors bought control of Eastern Airlines, and he became its president. In 1941, he suffered serious injuries when he was on an Eastern flight that crashed near Atlanta, killing seven passengers.

A year later, during World War II, he was on a special assignment to see General Douglas MacArthur when the B-17 plane that he was flying in crashed in the Pacific Ocean near Japanese-held islands. He and seven other men survived twenty-four grueling days on life rafts before they were rescued. One man died and the others barely survived while enduring starvation, dehydration, and exposure. Rickenbacker, who was fifty-two at the time, lost fifty-four pounds. After recovering from the ordeal, he continued to act as a military advisor during the war.

"Captain Eddie," as he liked to be called, remained Eastern's chief executive officer until 1959. He died in 1973 at the age of eighty-three and is buried in Green Lawn Cemetery in Columbus, Ohio.

THE IMMIGRANT DOUGHBOY
Army Private Abraham Krotoshinsky

Trapped for days without food, low on ammunition, and surrounded by enemy forces that were constantly attacking them, weakening doughboys kept battling their hearts out. But the number of killed, wounded, and captured mounted by the hour. The men knew they couldn't hold out much longer.

By the fifth day, all communication with headquarters had been cut off.

The commander who headed the besieged unit asked for a volunteer to do what dozens of men had died trying — sneak past the ironclad enemy cordon, deliver a vital message to headquarters, and return with a relief squad.

That's when Abraham Krotoshinsky — a Russian immigrant who had been a barber in New York City before enlisting in the U.S. Army — stepped forward. He knew the odds were stacked against him, but he had to try. It was the least he could do for his adopted country . . . and for his battle buddies.

Ironically, Krotoshinsky had fled his Russian homeland six years earlier to escape military service. He had despised the government because of its cruel and inhumane treatment of his fellow Jews. So he left the town of Plotzk (now known as Plock in what today is central Poland) and arrived in America in 1912, filled with the same hopes and dreams as millions of other immigrants.

Barely able to speak English, the nineteen-year-old was overwhelmed by the hustle and bustle of the big city, where he lived in a ramshackle apartment building. Although life was a struggle for him, he embraced America and enjoyed the freedoms he had never experienced under Russian domination. Finding work as a barber, he often told his customers in halting English, "This is a great land. This is my land."

When the United States entered the war in 1917, Krotoshinsky enlisted because, as he explained to his friends, "America is much more precious to me than the land of my birth. I am a patriot now."

Krotoshinsky was sent to Camp Upton on Long Island for training and assigned to the 77th Division. Known as the Metropolitan Division, the unit was made up mostly of New Yorkers, including poor but scrappy Jewish and Italian immigrants who were street-smart and tough. Many of its twenty-three thousand men had been drafted and were former Manhattan taxi drivers, Bronx tailors, Brooklyn factory workers, and Wall Street professionals. They chose the Statue of Liberty as the division's symbol and proudly wore a uniform patch of a golden Lady Liberty against a blue background.

After arriving in France in April 1918, the division soon gained respect from military leaders for its fighting ability, even though few men in the unit were professional soldiers. It was one of the reasons why the 77th was chosen in September to lead a direct attack through the Argonne Forest — the enemy's stronghold. Gloomy and forbidding, the Argonne was the largest expanse of woodland in northern France, stretching about forty-four miles long and ten miles wide from the Belgian frontier to the French town of Verdun. It was an area of dense woods, deep ravines, sheer cliffs, thick swamps, and muddy marshland — all of it chock-full of tangled underbrush, trailing vines, and sharp briars.

For four years, since the beginning of the war, the Germans had turned the Argonne into a seemingly unconquerable fortress. Their artillery covered approaches to every ravine and summit. Camouflaged machine gun nests were placed to command all roads, paths, and trails. Numerous lines of barbed-wire entanglements and chicken wire were interlaced among the trees. Lookout posts were built in treetops and ridges so observers could direct the fire of artillery and machine guns.

Like his comrades, Private Krotoshinsky, of Company K, 307th Infantry Regiment, was battle hardened by the time the 77th Division went over the top at 5:30 A.M. on September 26, 1918, in what is known as the Meuse-Argonne Offensive. Their mission was to rout the 2nd Landwehr Division of the German Army, which had been defending the Argonne. For the assault, the Americans had left behind their overcoats, blankets, tents, and rain gear so that they wouldn't be burdened by the extra weight. Each man carried a limited amount of food for the same reason.

In the cold rain, the doughboys slogged through the mud and thick bushes and tore down chicken wire and barbed wire. They endured snipers who were firing from treetops, concealed machine guns that were spewing bullets from every angle, and artillery and mortar rounds that were blowing up on all sides of them.

Despite the horrendous challenges, the men of the Metropolitan Division were making slow, steady progress into the Argonne. But casualties were swelling, too. "It hurts, no matter how hardened you are, to see your buddy right next to you bleeding and torn," Krotoshinsky told a comrade shortly before the operation.

The main way commanders on the battlefield communicated with headquarters in the rear was through runner posts. Soldiers who were stationed several hundred yards apart relayed messages much like a track team passes the baton in a relay race.

On October 2, several units of the 77th Division were ordered to break through enemy defenses and advance along a creek in a ravine to Charlevaux Mill. The orders were clear: Reach the objective regardless of casualties. Knowing how difficult it had been during the first week of the offensive in the Argonne, Major Charles Whittlesey, Commander of the 1st Battalion, told his superiors that his men would do their best, adding fretfully, "I don't know if you'll hear from us again."

Despite suffering many casualties, the 1st and 2nd Battalions, Private Krotoshinsky's Company K, and a few smaller units bravely fought their way deeper into the forest and reached their goal by 6 P.M. But the rest of the American forces were rebuffed by the Germans and had returned to their trenches, leaving the forward troops — all 687 of them — alone behind enemy lines.

The Germans seized the opportunity to close their breach to the rear of those doughboys and completely surrounded them. The Americans were now trapped in a wooded ravine roughly the size of four football fields in an area they called the "Pocket."

In a steady rain, Krotoshinsky and his buddies from Company K dug their own funk holes in the side of a hill and settled in to eat the last of their field rations. Word spread that two of the companies had been mobilized so quickly they hadn't had time to draw their rations. So Krotoshinsky and others shared their meager meals with those who had none. During the night, they all shivered in their funk holes, which were half full of water. Rest was difficult because enemy artillery kept bombarding the area.

By the next morning, the Germans had cut off all runner

lines by killing or capturing the runners. The only way left to communicate with headquarters for Whittlesey, who took command of the trapped men, was through carrier pigeons that were trained to fly back to their coops. The field commander wrote two messages describing the dire situation he and his men were in. He folded each message into a small canister attached to the leg of each carrier pigeon and released the birds.

Krotoshinsky and his comrades from Company K tried to reestablish the runner line toward the rear, but couldn't because the Germans had fortified the positions with machine guns.

Any thoughts of trying to retreat were banished. Whittlesey, who had been a New York attorney before the war, told his next two in command, Captain George McMurtry and Lieutenant Nelson Holderman, "Our mission is to hold our position in the Pocket at all costs. No falling back. Have this understood by every man in your command."

Later that afternoon, Krotoshinsky and the others ducked for cover after sniper fire erupted from all directions. When the shooting stopped, he heard enemy officers calling roll as they mustered their troops. He knew that meant only one thing: The Germans were going to attack. Minutes later, they charged the Pocket from four sides. Finding cover behind logs and rocks, Krotoshinsky and his battle buddies fired back, knowing that without a stout defense, they would end up prisoners or dead.

At 4:05 P.M. Whittlesey dispatched another carrier pigeon with a message that said, "Germans on cliff north of us in small numbers and have tried to envelope both flanks. Situation on left very serious." He asked for ammunition and grenades and reported that there had been nine men killed and one hundred forty wounded during the previous twenty-four hours.

Refusing to cave despite being outnumbered, the dough-boys beat back the enemy to live another day. That night, Krotoshinsky and others tended to the wounded, trying to keep them from crying out in pain to maintain silence. It was a heartbreaking task because the unit had few medical supplies. By now, more than half of the ninety-seven members of his own company were wounded.

Under cover of darkness, Whittlesey kept dispatching several runners, hoping someone would sneak past the enemy, reach headquarters, and return with reinforcements. But at daybreak it was obvious the effort had failed. Some runners staggered back wounded; the rest were not heard from again.

Whittlesey sent another message via carrier pigeon that said, in part, "Many wounded here whom we can't evacuate. Need rations badly."

There was no mess call the next morning, October 4, because there were no rations to eat. Although the wounded were suffering, so too were the able-bodied like Krotoshinsky, who were feeling the effects of the lack of food, water, and sleep, the cold nights, and the stress of fighting an enemy that had them surrounded.

Trying to ignore his misery, Krotoshinsky helped bury the dead. But the burial detail was soon halted by a barrage of enemy mortar rounds. Whittlesey then sent out a large patrol that climbed to the top of the ridge just in time to fend off Germans who were getting ready to lob grenades into the Pocket below.

At 10:55 A.M. Whittlesey sent a carrier pigeon with the message: "Germans are still around us, though in smaller numbers. We have been heavily shelled by mortar this morning. Present effective strength . . . about 235 . . . Cover bad if we advance up the hill and very difficult to move the wounded if we change position. Situation is cutting into our strength rapidly. Men are suffering from hunger and exposure; the wounded are in very bad condition. Cannot support be sent at once?"

What no one in the Pocket knew was that American forces *were* trying to rescue the men, but they were stymied by heavy German resistance.

Later in the afternoon, American artillery shells slammed into an enemy position on the ridge southeast of the Pocket. At first, Krotoshinsky and his comrades were elated to see the barrage. But then the rounds began landing closer and closer to the doughboys until the shells struck inside the Pocket.

As flying shrapnel tore into several unlucky troops, Krotoshinsky curled up in a funk hole, praying that the friendly fire wouldn't kill him. Some of the blasts caused funk holes to collapse, momentarily burying men. Other explosions destroyed the trees and dense brush that had provided the men some cover from the enemy gunners.

As the artillery continued to pound the Pocket, Major Whittlesey frantically wrote a message, attached it to his last carrier pigeon — named Cher Ami (French for "dear friend") — and hoped the bird would reach headquarters. The message said: "We are along the road parallel to 276.4. Our own artillery is dropping a barrage directly on us. For heaven's sake, stop it!"

Somewhat disoriented from all the shelling, Cher Ami flew to a low branch on a nearby tree. The doughboys yelled encouragement to the small bird, which had successfully delivered eleven messages during earlier action at Verdun. When she wouldn't fly off, the men threw stones at her to convince her to leave.

Cher Ami finally took flight. But the Germans along the ridge spotted her and, knowing she was carrying a message, began shooting at her. As the Americans watched in dismay, Cher Ami was struck by a bullet and began a slow spiral toward the ground. But just when the men thought their last appeal for help had failed, she began flying again and managed to flutter beyond the range of enemy fire. Thirty minutes later, the friendly fire ceased.

The survivors had rightly assumed that Cher Ami had delivered the message that led to the halt of the artillery. What they didn't know was that the heroic bird had flown twenty-five miles to headquarters after enemy bullets had blinded one eye, tore a hole in her breast, and nearly shot off her right leg, which was hanging to her body by a tendon.

Unfortunately, the shelling had claimed the lives of more than thirty Americans. Bearing such a huge loss from their own artillery had left the men in the Pocket demoralized. However, their spirits picked up when they heard American biplanes flying overhead. Whittlesey instructed his men to set out two large white marking panels so that the pilots might see the trapped men's exact location through the thick forest and possibly drop supplies soon.

Buoyed with such hope, Krotoshinsky and the others turned back a vicious German grenade attack late in the afternoon. That night, some of the men tried to draw water from a small pond just outside the Pocket, but German machine guns mowed down most of them. The few men who returned with freshwater gave it to the wounded.

The next day, October 5, Krotoshinsky helped bury the dead. The grim task took his mind off the hunger pangs and the thirst that had consumed him throughout another restless night.

During the day, he and the others caught occasional glimpses of planes dropping small packages. But the surrounded troops were well hidden in the ravine, making it virtually impossible for the pilots to find them even with the white panels. Most of the desperately needed packages of rations, ammo, and medical supplies landed just outside the Pocket and into the hands of the enemy. Soldiers who attempted to retrieve packages were gunned down before they could reach them. The news grew grimmer when two planes attempting air drops were shot down.

After more than forty-eight hours without food, Krotoshinsky joined others in foraging among the brush for roots, berries, and nuts that could relieve the hunger pangs. However, most of their time was spent fending off repeated attacks throughout the day. McMurtry and Holderman both suffered bad combat injuries, but they continued to encourage their men.

The constant fighting left the doughboys with a dwindling supply of ammunition. Of their nine machine guns, only two were still working. As night fell, Krotoshinsky and a handful of others crawled out to the closest German bodies and stripped them of bullets, rifles, and anything else that the survivors could use.

The men entered their fourth night trapped in the Pocket, their third night without food, water, or decent shelter from the cold rain.

Krotoshinsky couldn't sleep much because the wounded were moaning in agony. Everyone had given up trying to keep them silent. In the woods, just beyond the Pocket, he heard enemy soldiers laughing and taunting the Americans. Some of the Germans shouted in English that they were feasting on bacon, bread, and chocolate taken from the air-dropped bundles.

On October 6 — the fourth full day of the siege — the survivors were once again under continuous trench mortar, machine gun, and sniper fire. By now it was too dangerous and too exhausting to bury the dead. Whittlesey wanted his starving, fatigued troops to conserve as much of their energy as possible to repel the enemy. During lulls in the fighting, the desperate men removed the bandages from their dead comrades and reused them on the wounded, who were barely clinging to life.

The following morning, it was discovered that eight soldiers had sneaked off on their own in search of dropped packages. They still hadn't returned by late in the afternoon, and their fate was unknown.

But then from an enemy-held position in the woods emerged a lone soldier in an American uniform. He was limping on a cane and holding a stick with a white cloth tied to it. He was Private Lowell Hollingshead, one of the nine missing men. Brought to the commanding officers, Hollingshead said that four were killed and the rest were wounded and captured. He said he was released on condition that he give Whittlesey a handwritten letter from Lieutenant Heinrich Prinz, commander of the German unit that had captured the private. The letter said:

"The bearer of this present, Private Lowell R. Hollingshead, has been taken by us. He refused to give the German Intelligence Officer any answer to his questions, and is quite an honorable fellow, doing honor to his Fatherland in the strictest sense of the word.

"He has been charged against his will, believing that he is doing wrong to his country to carry forward this present letter to the officer in charge of the battalion of the 77th

Division, with the purpose to recommend this commander to surrender with his forces, as it would be quite useless to resist any more, in view of the present conditions.

"The suffering of your wounded men can be heard over here in the German lines, and we are appealing to your humane sentiments to stop. A white flag shown by one of your men will tell us that you agree with these conditions. Please treat Private Hollingshead as an honorable man. He is quite a soldier. We envy you.

"The German Commanding Officer"

Despite the letter's courteous tone and reasoned approach, Whittlesey — with McMurtry and Holderman agreeing — decided the best response, and the only one, was to not give any response. The major even ordered that the white panels on the ground be removed immediately because he didn't want the Germans to mistake them for a sign of surrender.

When Krotoshinsky and the others learned about the letter, they found renewed vigor to resist the enemy. Even though the men were emotionally and physically drained, they began swearing at the unseen Germans, and defiantly shouted such things as, "If you want us, then come and get us!" "We'll never surrender!" "We're too tough to quit!"

In response, the Germans launched their heaviest attack yet, flinging a salvo of grenades and raking the Pocket with mortars and a steady stream of machine gun fire. With what little strength and ammo they had left, the doughboys fought with fury, believing it was their last stand. Krotoshinsky figured that if he was going to die, he was going to take as many Germans as he could with him to the grave.

Amazingly, the Americans warded off the latest assault as they had all the previous ones. But the number of dead and wounded continued to climb. And without food, water, medical supplies, and ammunition, the survivors knew they couldn't hold out much longer.

Someone had to get past the enemy and make it to headquarters and return with a relief squad. Whittlesey asked for a volunteer. Krotoshinsky stepped forward. He was fully aware that thirty-six men had tried over the previous five days and all had been captured, killed, or had turned back because they were too wounded.

At first, Krotoshinsky figured he had nothing to lose. Hungry, thirsty, and weak, he thought that if he were shot, at least he would be put out of his misery. But once he was given his orders, he felt a burst of faith that he would succeed when all others had failed.

It was overcast and gloomy when he cautiously set out on what most everyone considered a suicide mission. Treading as lightly as possible on the fallen leaves, Krotoshinsky flitted from one tree to the next, hoping no snipers or patrols would see him.

As he neared one of the enemy lines, he caught sight of an overweight German officer who was walking toward him but hadn't spotted him yet. The only nearby cover for Krotoshinsky was a small bush. Realizing that he might still be exposed if he tried to crouch behind it, he sprawled on the ground, face down and arms out, and pretended to be dead. The area was already littered with bodies, both Americans and Germans.

Hearing the *crunch, crunch, crunch* of footsteps getting louder, Krotoshinsky remained motionless and wondered if the officer would ignore him or put a bullet in his head to make sure he was dead. Krotoshinsky held his breath. His heart pounded so furiously he worried it would give him away.

As the officer walked within a few feet of him, the prone soldier was running out of air and his lungs were starting to burn. He knew he had maybe ten seconds left before he would need to breathe, which might give him away.

The officer walked right up to him . . . and then stepped on Krotoshinsky's fingers.

The soldier stifled a scream as the man's full weight mashed the fingers into the ground. Krotoshinsky remained silent, but he reflexively sucked in some air because of the pain. Without slowing down, the officer continued on his way.

Krotoshinsky didn't move. He could hear other footsteps nearby, so he lay among the dead for several hours until his ears detected nothing but gunfire from deeper in the woods. When he finally got up, he crouched low and looked for a way out of the Pocket.

But then he was spotted by a sniper, who fired on him. That brought other Germans to the area, and they began shooting at him. Finding untapped energy, Krotoshinsky darted into the woods and lost one patrol only to be shot at by another. He was struck in the arm and leg, but he kept moving. Under constant fire the rest of the day, Krotoshinsky assumed that at any moment, he would be felled by a fatal bullet. Aside from impending death, he thought of nothing else but the need to reach headquarters. His home, his family, his friends were all forgotten. He just had to make it.

For ten frightening hours, Krotoshinsky played a deadly game of cat and mouse with German scouts and snipers. At times he sprinted through machine gun fire. Other times he inched along flat on his stomach. More than once he pretended to be a corpse. He doubled back, retraced his route, and made several detours in an effort to throw his pursuers off his track. Eventually, he found a break in the enemy cordon.

It was starting to get dark when Krotoshinsky skirted past the last German trench and reached No Man's Land. As he crawled near an American trench, he faced a new dilemma: How could he convince the soldiers he was one of them? He was coming from the German lines, he spoke English with a thick accent, and he didn't know the password for the day. It would be easy for soldiers to mistake him for a spy and shoot before he could explain who he was. He decided to call out "Hello!" several times, because the Germans seldom used that word when they tried to speak English.

Wary that he was the enemy, several soldiers pointed their rifles at him as he told his story. Then they escorted him to headquarters, where he delivered Major Whittlesey's message, gave his unit's exact position, and told of the terrible conditions the men were in. "We need medical attention, food, and water — and reinforcements," he said.

After he was given something to eat — the first real food he had swallowed in five days — he was examined by a doctor and asked if he was strong enough to guide a relief squad back into the Pocket.

Although he was exhausted, he replied, "Yes. I know the way."

The squad gathered up rations, ammo, and medical supplies and then followed Krotoshinsky as he led them in the dark past the German defenses and to his starving, wounded, and desperate comrades. The arrival was greeted by the survivors with surprise, but no cheers. They were too exhausted and weak. But their faces lit up because for the first time in nearly a week, they knew they might actually survive.

The little immigrant New York barber had accomplished what so many others had died trying — helping save the lives of those who became known forever as members of The Lost Battalion.

After the enemy's cordon around the Pocket was breached, more American forces joined the relief squad and eventually drove the Germans out of the forest as part of the much larger Meuse-Argonne Offensive. The overall assault lasted 47 days, involved 1.2 million American troops, and effectively brought an end to the war.

Of the 554 men who were trapped in the Pocket, only 194 walked out on their own power. The rest had been wounded (190), killed (107), or were listed as missing in action or captured (63). After completing his mission, Krotoshinsky was treated in a hospital for his wounds and recovered relatively quickly.

Cher Ami, the wounded carrier pigeon, initially survived her wounds thanks to the diligent efforts of army medics. They couldn't save her right leg, so they carved a small wooden one for her instead. The valiant bird lived for another eight months but finally succumbed to her wounds. Before her death, she received France's prestigious Croix de Guerre. Cher Ami's body was later mounted by a taxidermist and enshrined in the Smithsonian Institution in Washington, D.C.

For their leadership during the siege in the Pocket, Major Whittlesey, Captain McMurtry, and Captain Holderman were awarded the Medal of Honor.

For the courage he displayed in his perilous journey, Krotoshinsky was given the Distinguished Service Cross, which was personally presented by General John Pershing.

Krotoshinsky returned to New York, where he was hailed a hero and eventually became an American citizen. But by 1927, he was unemployed and penniless with a wife and two small children to support. After a story about Krotoshinsky's plight appeared in the newspaper, President Calvin Coolidge personally signed an executive order giving the veteran a position as a clerk in a Manhattan post office. Krotoshinsky worked there the rest of his life until his death in 1953 at the age of sixty.

THE FIGHTING EIGHTH

The 8th Illinois National Guard/
370th U.S. Army Infantry

About four hundred thousand African-Americans served in the military in World War I, mostly as laborers and support personnel. When the United States entered the war, there were twenty thousand black troops who were already in uniform. Half were in segregated regiments in the regular army — the 9th and 10th Cavalry and the 24th and 25th Infantry Regiment. The other half were in predominantly black National Guard units, including the 8th Illinois Regiment, the 15th New York Regiment, the 9th Separate Battalion of Ohio, and the 1st Separate Battalion of the District of Columbia, among others. This is the story of the men of the 8th Illinois — the country's only African-American regiment that was called into service with a complete complement of black officers from colonel to second lieutenant.

*   *   *

To the 2,166 black officers and enlisted men of the 8th Illinois National Guard, there was at least one good thing about going to war: It was an opportunity to show their country that they were loyal Americans and tough soldiers. Even more important, it was their chance to knock down racial barriers and gain greater respect from whites, which the African-Americans hoped would lead to equality in everyday life.

But before they could fire their first bullet in combat, they had to fight racism in the United States. After the unit was called to active duty on July 25, 1917, the men were supposed to train at Camp Logan near Houston, Texas. For nearly three months, however, they were forced to work out at their armory in Chicago because officials in Texas refused to allow black soldiers from any other state to train within its borders.

So under the leadership of Colonel Franklin A. Denison and his officers, the men, who called themselves "The Fighting Eighth," drilled in the armory. They resolved that they would become fine soldiers despite the racial hindrance and that they would surprise the military world with their fighting spirit.

Finally, in October, after pressure from the War Department, the black soldiers from Illinois were allowed to train at Camp Logan. In a letter to his congregation in Chicago, the unit's chaplain, Captain William S. Braddan, wrote, "It's up to us to convert the whites of Houston from hate to love; to make people who regard the regiment as a bunch of lawless men realize that we would wade through the fires of Hell to gain and hold for our race a large place in the sun; and to dispel all doubts relative to our loyalty, discipline, and patriotism."

The unit, one of the army's four African-American regiments, arrived in France in April 1918 and was given a new designation — the 370th Infantry. It was then the troops learned they wouldn't be fighting with their fellow Americans, but with the French Army, which was in dire need of replacement soldiers after four years of war. The segregated U.S. Army was more than willing to loan the French all the black soldiers they wanted. As a result, the African-American combat units were divided up piecemeal and attached to various French divisions.

The men of the 370th were ordered to turn in their American equipment with which they had trained for months. They were issued French rifles, pistols, helmets, machine guns, horses, wagons, and coats. The troops even received the same rations given to French soldiers, which consisted of food sufficient for two meals per day compared to the three that white American soldiers received.

"The U.S. Army certainly doesn't want us," was a common complaint among the men. Despite having to deal with unfamiliar French arms, equipment, and language, the black troops were soon combat ready.

As part of the 10th French Army, the men of the 370th settled into the trenches of St. Mihiel — the first American soldiers to do so. As distant enemy guns boomed, Braddan told his comrades, "Fellows, you stand as pioneers on the frontier of your race's progress. If you fail, the hands on the dial of your race's progress will be pushed back fifty years. The whites over there [in the U.S.] are expecting you to fail, because you are officered by [black] men. Now go to it and show them how, when led by your own officers, you can and will charge Hell with a bucket of water!"

One of the men shouted back, "Captain, we will make good and return with honor or we will not return at all!"

While the unit was being moved from one hot spot to another along the Western Front, the army replaced Colonel Denison with a white officer, Colonel T. A. Roberts. The troops were outraged when it was reported that for the return address on his private mail, Roberts would write, "The White Hope in a Black Regiment." They became suspicious that the army was starting to purge the unit of black officers when two other white officers were brought in.

The troops might have felt the sting of racism in the military, but they didn't feel it in the French countryside. As they passed hundreds of villagers, the soldiers were met with shouts of *Vive les Américains! Vive la France!* ("Long live the Americans! Long live France!")

During these marches, Braddan saw several churches that the enemy had destroyed. He thought, *What devils these Germans must be to emblazon on their belt plates "Gott Mit Uns"* [God is with us] *and then desecrate God's temples.*

Acts of bravery and valor were common in the unit. While conducting a raid, Lieutenant Harvey Taylor was shot

six times, but he refused to stay down and instead continued to lead his men in a successful mission. Private Spirley
Irby was carrying messages back and forth under withering enemy fire, and even though he was badly wounded,
he crawled to headquarters with vital information. (He
would later be awarded the Distinguished Service Cross for
his actions.) Private Alfred Williamson, of the Medical
Detachment, was assigned to duty at the first-aid station,
but instead accompanied the attacking troops so he could
tend to the wounded. During the advance, he constantly
came under enemy fire while treating the fallen.

Acting as an ammunition carrier, Private Arthur
Johnson received a painful injury in the back from a shell
fragment, yet still carried out his duties. While hauling
ammunition, he spotted a wounded comrade in No Man's
Land. Despite heavy enemy fire and the pain from his own
wound, Johnson lugged the nearly unconscious soldier
through flying bullets for nearly a mile to a first-aid station
and then continued his job of delivering ammo to machine
gunners.

In a letter to his congregation back home, Braddan
wrote, "It's a safe bet that when you receive this letter, we
will be used as shock troops, leading the charge against the
enemy and, after drawing their fire, return to the rear. This
we will do for three or four days, then go to the rear, rest for
two days, replenish our regiment, and go at them again.
When you hear of how we're being used, don't protest,
because it's a glorious calling — and none but the brave fight

like this. While it's the most dangerous, it's the most glorious. This is war. *C'est la Guerre."*

In September, the regiment moved to positions in the Soissons sector. Some of its companies pushed forward to positions in front of Mont des Signes and engaged in bloody battles that led to overrunning several of the enemy's strongest embattlements.

During the French-led counteroffensive, the 370th captured nearly 1,900 prisoners as well as enemy artillery, including dozens of cannons, trench mortars, and machine guns. The battlefield teemed with heroic efforts.

Sergeant Matthew Jenkins led a platoon that captured enemy machine gun positions and used the weapons against the Germans. The small group of Americans held their position for thirty-six long hours without food or water until reinforcements arrived. (For his leadership in this capture, Sergeant Jenkins received both the Distinguished Service Cross and the Croix de Guerre.)

During the action at Mont des Singes, several companies were dangerously low of food. Corporal Emmett Thompson volunteered to take charge of a detail to secure rations. Enduring heavy shelling and machine gun fire, he and his men ran back and forth, hauling needed supplies to hungry troops. Even though half his men in the detail were wounded or killed, Thompson continued to get supplies to his comrades until he fell from exhaustion. (He, too, earned the Distinguished Service Cross.)

When his platoon commander was killed, Private Charles T. Monroe took charge and directed his men to continue firing their trench mortars even though enemy artillery had targeted them. At times, the shelling was so intense that the troops' mortars were temporarily buried by dirt and debris from the explosions. Monroe and his men worked unceasingly in getting the weapons back into action. He himself was buried by the explosion of a shell, but after his comrades dug him out, he continued to lead them, refusing to move to safer ground.

When Sergeant Lester Fossie saw a messenger get shot by an enemy sniper in an exposed area, Fossie immediately went to his rescue. Ignoring machine gun and sniper fire, he zigzagged out into No Man's Land, picked up the wounded messenger, and brought him to safety at the company headquarters. (Fossie was later awarded the Distinguished Service Cross.)

Eventually, the men of the 370th were loaded into a hundred trucks at Mareuil-sur-Ourcq to face the well-trained German troops called the Prussian Guards. Noted for its spiked helmets, the pride of the German Army was entrenched along the famous Hindenburg Line — a ninety-mile-long defensive position designed to protect Germany from invasion. The Guards had boasted that it was impossible for the Allies to get past them.

In a letter home, Lieutenant Colonel Otis B. Duncan — the highest-ranking black officer in the U.S. Army and the recipient of the Croix de Guerre — described some of the fighting: "Beginning September 27, 1918, we sailed into them and drove them back to the Ailette Canal, where they made a stand, facing us not 50 yards away. The fighting here was fierce. The Germans had placed barbed-wire entanglements in the canal, but we avoided these with pontoon bridges and continued our drive. We reached what was known as Mont des Signes, or 'Monkey Mountain.' We took up our position here between 'Monkey Mountain' and the German line, near a narrow-gauge railroad. Here we encountered more concrete emplacements, dugouts, and barbed wire. In getting to the Germans, every man had to climb up on that railroad embankment, where we were fair marks for any kind of shell the Germans sent over. Naturally, we lost many of our men."

On September 28, Colonel Roberts sent for Braddan and complained about the troops' performance. "Captain, these men are a bunch of cowards," Roberts claimed. "The officers are no better. They don't seem to have any spirit. They don't shout when they go over the top."

Braddan was aghast. "I don't know what you're talking about, Colonel, but I do know that a braver bunch of men never got together. Do you realize we've lost a hundred men a day, and we've been up here over a week?"

"Well, none have been killed."

"Sir, I have buried forty."

"Well, that's what soldiers are for — to be killed and wounded."

"Very well, sir, but when they go bravely forward to their death or to be wounded, it ill becomes the commanding officer to brand them cowards and quitters."

Braddan saluted, spun on his heels, and left, fuming mad that the army had replaced a competent black commander who was praised by French generals with a white prejudiced officer who could care less about the casualties among his black soldiers.

Furious, the chaplain wrote his congregation back in Chicago, "How often have I thought how inconsistent for my government to send these willing subjects to Europe to fight autocracy, and for democracy, while it denied the same to its most loyal and patriotic subjects, the Negro."

From September 27 to October 4, the 370th was subjected to severe shelling and murderous fire from numerous machine guns and rifles. Wrote Braddan, "Missiles of death were everywhere falling; death was all around us, dead Frenchmen, Germans, and horses. Equipment of every description lay in the recently evacuated trenches. The sight was appalling, the scent nauseating. While the Germans were shelling our boys, we went out and buried fallen comrades in No Man's Land."

During this time, patrols from the regiment's 2nd and 3rd Battalions were out between the lines night and day, locating and destroying machine gun nests.

Colonel Roberts deliberately sent out troops on a mission during the day, even though orders from higher up called for it to take place at night. As a result, the unit suffered heavy casualties — nearly one hundred wounded or killed. Roberts blamed the debacle on the black officers, claiming they went out on the mission without the support of artillery. When the truth was learned, however, the French 10th Army relieved Colonel Roberts of his command of the 370th, citing as its reason that he lacked initiative and the ability to lead under fire.

Meanwhile, racist American soldiers circulated pamphlets among the French meant to demean and degrade African-American soldiers. Called "Secret Information Concerning Black American Troops," the pamphlets urged French civilians to avoid all social contact with African-Americans beyond military operations. This persistent campaign to discredit blacks and spread American racism in France was denounced by the French Chamber of Deputies, which ordered the collection and destruction of the inflammatory pamphlets. The French government passed a resolution supporting the rights of all men; condemning religious, class, or racial prejudice; and affirming social equality and equal protection under the law. Bigoted American officers condemned the resolution because they feared black troops would demand this same social freedom after they returned to the United States.

If the men of the 370th felt the pain of racism, they didn't let it interfere with their missions. They were determined to carry out orders to seize Laon, an important hilltop town that had been terrorized by the Germans during four merciless years of occupation. But lying between the Americans and their objective were the Ailette River and the Mortier Woods, all fortified by the Germans. The Blue Devils, a crack French division that the African-American troops had just relieved, declared it was impossible to oust the enemy in Laon.

But on October 13, the black soldiers became the first Americans to wrest control of the French fortress town from the Germans. After four years of domination, cruelty, and intimidation, thousands of grateful civilians hugged and kissed each other and every soldier they saw.

Two days later, the regiment joined their French comrades in the pursuit of the fleeing Germans. By now, after weeks of nonstop fighting, many of the black troops were wearing torn and ragged uniforms and shoes with holes. Everyone was haggard, unshaven, and half dead from a lack of sleep. Yet they were in good spirits because they had the enemy on the ropes.

In a span of thirty days, the 370th had cleared Monkey Mountain of every German, pushed the enemy out of Laon, routed them from the trenches of Aisne, and made them wade across the Ailette River back toward Germany. The black troops were so close that many Germans fled in panic, leaving behind their guns in the Mortier Woods, and even their beer and whiskey.

The month-long battle that defeated the Germans came at a price for the 370th: four hundred wounded, forty-five killed. The dead were buried in a cemetery in the town of Chambery. "There among five hundred German graves lie the greatest number of Negroes buried in one place in all of France," wrote Braddan.

Toward the end of October and into November, the black soldiers steadily and relentlessly pushed the Germans back until the enemy went into a full-scale retreat. In hot pursuit in a steady rain, the Americans captured artillery batteries, machine gun nests, a railroad supply line, and countless prisoners while fighting the enemy's frantic rearguard action.

In the final drive against the Germans in the French sector, the 370th advanced as much as twenty miles a day. The troops never relented, fighting up to the very last hour of the war. In fact, they fought the final battle, capturing a German wagon train of fifty wagons and crews on November 11.

After the armistice, Braddan had time to reflect on his service to the men of the 370th and to his country. He recalled a difficult march he and the troops made in early September when they trekked for hours in silence. "It was a . . . silence of the most nerve-racking kind, nothing but thoughts of home," he wrote. "We were marching light without packs, just two blankets, gun and ammunition, canteen and gas mask. Yet that equipment, as light as it was, seemed to bend us double.

"I have often thought that the thing that weighed us down was the consciousness that the weight of a doting race had staked its future on us. Our willingness and ability to make good was weighing upon our shoulders. If we failed in this supreme test, the entire race would fail.

And more than one of us swore that very night, 'We shall not fail.'"

Among the men of the 370th, twenty-one earned the Distinguished Service Cross, sixty-eight were awarded the Croix de Guerre, and one received the Distinguished Service Medal, making the regiment one of the most decorated in the entire United States Army.

On February 17, 1919, the men arrived back home in Chicago to great fanfare. The Chicago Defender — a newspaper covering the African-American community — called the return of the city's black doughboys "a day of wild rejoicing." The paper estimated that four hundred thousand cheering people lined Michigan Avenue as the regiment — still referred to as the 8th Illinois — marched by the reviewing stand, which was filled with white and black dignitaries. Offices and stores had closed for the day, and sixty thousand exuberant Chicagoans jammed the Coliseum, an exposition hall on the city's South Side, to welcome the unit.

The black troops felt optimistic that because of their service to their country, life would be much better for African-Americans. They were buoyed by former President Theodore Roosevelt's words for returning black soldiers: "I expect that as a result of this great war, intended to secure a greater justice internationally among the people of mankind, we shall apply at home the lessons that we have been learning and helping teach abroad; that we shall work sanely, not foolishly, but resolutely, toward securing a just and fairer treatment in this country of colored people, basing that treatment upon the only safe rule to be followed in American life: of treating each individual accordingly as his conduct or her conduct require you to treat them."

Unfortunately, racism was as strong as ever in American society after the war. A reported seventy-eight blacks were lynched in 1919. Competition for jobs between blacks and whites grew stronger, fueling fear, mistrust, and hatred.

For the veterans of the 8th Illinois, their quest for social justice faltered just five months after their return to their beloved city. It happened during a summer heat wave when Chicagoans had flocked to the city's beaches along Lake Michigan. On July 27, a black youth inadvertently swam beyond his segregated beach and into a whites-only area. Outraged whites threw rocks at him, causing him to drown. When white policemen called to the scene made no attempt to take any suspects into custody, tension mounted until it erupted into a full-scale riot.

Mobs of white men assaulted blacks while, in retaliation, blacks beat up white peddlers and merchants. White gunmen sped through Chicago's predominantly black neighborhoods, known as the Black Belt, shooting indiscriminately and setting houses and stores ablaze. From their fire escapes and windows, blacks, many of them veterans of the war, returned fire.

The violence lasted five days before National Guardsmen from the state capital in Springfield were called in to help restore order. The mayhem resulted in the deaths of twenty-three blacks and fifteen whites and injuries to more than five hundred people, and left an estimated one thousand black families homeless.

Although not as deadly or destructive as Chicago's, similar racially motivated riots erupted in nearly three dozen cities during the next weeks in what is forever known as Red Summer.

For the men who put their lives on the line fighting for America, the bloody turmoil was a heartbreaking setback to their hopes for racial equality. Braddan, who penned his wartime memoirs called Under Fire with the 370th Infantry, wrote in 1920, "[We were] crusaders of democracy, bearing that to the stricken French which we ourselves had never enjoyed in the land of the free, and the home of the brave."

THE DEVIL DOG
Marine Gunner William Nice

Torpedo off the starboard bow!" a sailor shouted with alarm.

"Another torpedo off the starboard stern!" yelled another.

Marine Gunner William Nice, who was in charge of three guns on the troopship *DeKalb,* peered into the moonlit Atlantic and spotted two German U-boats. Rushing from one gun placement to the other, he directed his men to fire on the submarines. Within minutes, the rounds scored a direct hit on one U-boat and drove the other off.

Luckily, both torpedoes had missed the ship — but just barely.

To his men, who were among the first Marines heading to France to fight in the war, he said, "Boys, that was a close call. Expect many more once we get to the front."

The barrel-chested thirty-five-year-old career Marine (whose rank was that of a chief warrant officer) had experienced many close calls since he enlisted twelve years earlier in 1905. He had fought in previous hotspots in Haiti, Dominican Republic, Mexico, Nicaragua, and Cuba. Now, in June 1917, he and his comrades of the 49th Company, 5th Regiment were steaming across the Atlantic for what he termed "the greatest adventure of our lives."

Most of the men under his command were seasoned veterans who lived by the unit motto, "We tame the tough ones and toughen the tame ones." They were ready to prove they were the best fighting force in the world. He didn't need any convincing. He already knew that. So when the Marines arrived in France as the first major American military unit, Nice and his fellow leathernecks were itching to take on the hated *Boches*, an insulting French term for German soldiers.

But for all the bravado and training and experience, the Marines weren't prepared for the amount of blood they would shed.

Before dawn on June 6, 1918, the Marines were poised to launch an all-out assault on the German-held Belleau Wood. First they needed to secure Hill 142 on their left and the town of Bouresches on their right. So Nice and the other 250 men of the 49th Company, who were under the command of Captain George Hamilton, left behind much of their gear except their twenty-pound combat packs. They loaded up on extra hand grenades and ammunition and made sure they each had their gas mask.

Joined by the 67th Company, the leathernecks spread out along an 800-yard line in front of the low, pine-covered hill that for many months had been controlled by the enemy. In this case, the enemy happened to be two of the most highly trained units in the German Army. The goal of capturing the hill was even more daunting, because the Marines would have to cross open wheat fields, meadows, woods, and shallow ravines where German machine guns were already set up.

Many will die today, Nice thought. *I don't intend to be one of them.*

With bayonets fixed, the Marines moved forward in the mist. The sun had just peeked over the horizon, casting a reddish-orange glow on the dewy wheat and turning the poppy fields a bright crimson that reminded Nice of blood. As they began their advance, he gazed at the men on his left and right. Seeing the fortitude in their eyes, he felt confident they would reach their objective. He had seen that look many times before in previous battles in other lands.

Nice and his men had walked about fifty yards in the open toward a group of trees without any sign of the enemy when suddenly the morning quiet was shattered by ear-pounding explosions from German artillery shells landing among the Marines. The bombardment was accompanied by intense fire from Maxim heavy machine guns along the front edge of the woods.

Nice and everyone else around him dropped to the ground, hoping the wheat stalks and poppies would offer some cover, however minimal it was. He had never heard so many machine guns roaring at once. It was deafening.

"Fire at will!" Nice shouted to the men in the two platoons he commanded. But he wondered if they could hear him above the din. Looking through the wheat, he noticed that the Germans manning the machine guns had a clear view of the Marines. *This is a killing field,* he thought.

Firing at their full five hundred rounds per minute, the Maxims laid down a wall of bullets, making it virtually impossible for anyone to move. Several machine guns were aimed so low that the bullets riddled the backpacks of many Marines, like Nice, who were hugging the ground. German snipers hiding in nearby trees began picking off the prone leathernecks.

Above the noise, Nice could hear the wounded crying out for stretcher bearers and first-aid men. *We're dead if we stay here much longer,* he thought. Glancing over to his left, he saw Captain Hamilton yank six men to their feet and lead them on a charge into the woods directly at the machine guns. *It's our only chance,* Nice thought.

Taking a couple of deep breaths, Nice rose and, while crouched, ran over to the men in his platoon who hadn't been killed in the initial onslaught, and shouted, "Follow me! We have to get 'em before they cut us all down!"

The Marines rose and, yelling at the top of their lungs, sprinted into the woods. Those who weren't gunned down leaped into the machine gun nests and attacked the Germans in hand-to-hand combat. All Nice could think about was thrusting his bayonet through every machine gunner he encountered, refusing to show any mercy to those who had been mowing down his comrades.

Enemy fire seemed to be coming from behind every tree. But Nice and a handful of his men pressed on until they were slowed up by a machine gun nest in a wooded depression that was spurting out a constant stream of deadly fire. *We have to take it out if we're going to advance,* he thought.

While the enemy gunners in the nest were concentrating on the Marines advancing in front of them, Nice and sixteen men low-crawled off to the side and then sneaked up behind the enemy. Just as the leathernecks were about to shoot, a German looked behind and saw them. Throwing up his hands, he shouted *"Kamerad!"* [comrade] and surrendered. His fellow soldiers turned around and also gave up — all twenty-six of them.

Once the Germans were disarmed, Nice ordered six of his men to march them back to the American lines. Then he and the rest hunted for other nests. At one nest, they discovered two machine guns that had been firing rounds without being manned. The guns were set up at the top of a deep depression and were operated by weights attached by lanyards (strong cords) to the triggers. Strings of ammunition containing one thousand rounds were fed by another set of weights.

By now the Marines had overwhelmed the Germans, bursting through their defensive line and pushing over the top of Hill 142 and its flanking slope.

Meanwhile, Captain Hamilton had led dozens of his men six hundred yards beyond the hill and was now catching fire from three sides. Not only that, but American artillery rounds were getting uncomfortably close to them. "We've gone too far!" he told Nice. "We must get back to our objective, reorganize, and dig in."

Following Hamilton, Nice crawled through a drainage ditch filled with cold water and reeds as machine gun bullets zipped inches above his back. He, Hamilton, and most of the others eventually returned to the top of Hill 142.

Reinforcements soon joined the 49th Company on the north slope just in time to fight off repeated counterattacks by the Germans. During one enemy assault, Second Lieutenant Vernon Somers was struck by several bullets while leading a squad in a flanking movement designed to cut off an enemy advance.

Seeing the officer lying on the ground and badly bleeding in the open thirty yards from the Americans' hastily dug trench, Nice leaped into action. Bent over at the waist, he sprinted toward his fallen comrade. When Nice reached him, Somers groaned, "They got me good, Gunner." His entire torso was covered in blood.

"Don't give up," Nice said. "I'll get you out of here."

Nice picked him up, draped him over his shoulder, and hurried toward the American line. Nice was halfway there when an enemy bullet slammed into his back, sending him and Somers crashing to the ground. Gritting his teeth, Nice scrambled to his feet, lifted the officer, and staggered forward until he collapsed short of the Marines' trench. Several soldiers then dragged the pair to safety.

Both of them were put on stretchers and taken to the first-aid station in the rear. After examining Nice, a medic told him, "That's a nasty wound, but you're lucky. It's not fatal, and the bullet isn't near any vital organ. You'll have to spend the night here, and then we'll move you to a hospital in the morning so they can get the bullet out."

"What about Somers?" Nice asked. "Is he going to make it?"

The medic shook his head. "He died a few minutes ago."

Nice spent a restless, painful night. The next morning he was told he would be transported to a hospital later in the day. *I have no intention of being taken to the hospital,* he told himself. *My boys need me. Heck, if I'm sent to the hospital I might end up with some other unit after I recover. I want to stay here and fight with my boys, and I'm going to do it.*

Even though the bullet was still lodged in his back, Nice slipped out of the medical station and returned to Hill 142. It was then that he learned from his close friend, Lieutenant Chuck Connor, the cost of capturing and holding the hill. "Five times the *Boches* counterattacked, but we beat them back each time," Connor told him. "Their dead were piling up, but our losses were heavy, too. We ourselves, the 49th, lost sixty-two percent of our company. Ninety percent of our officers and fifty percent of our enlisted men were either captured or killed."

Nice shook his head in dismay over the grim news. "It could have been worse if it hadn't been for you, Chuck," he said. "I heard you led some of our men in a bayonet charge against a machine gun, captured it, and turned it against the enemy."

Connor shrugged and replied, "All in a day's work."

But the Marines' work was only just beginning. Despite the physically and emotionally draining battle over Hill 142, they now had to capture Bouresches, a village of about one thousand that was located near the southeastern end of Belleau Wood and under German control.

Dodging enemy artillery and disregarding the pain from the bullet in his back, Nice led his platoons in the Marine's first assault on the town. Although his unit suffered many casualties, other platoons were wiped out completely in fierce fighting.

During lulls in the battle, Red Cross aid men on both sides ran out into the open and treated the wounded without getting shot at out of respect for the fallen. Late in the afternoon, Nice held his fire as he watched a German first-aid team carry a stretcher back toward enemy lines. A blanket covered what appeared to be a soldier whose knees were drawn up. Just then a gust blew back the edge of the blanket, revealing a weapon. "That's no soldier!" Nice shouted to his men. "That's a Maxim they're carrying! Fire at will!"

The Marines gunned them down, but the sneaky trick the Germans attempted put an end to the unwritten pact that both sides wouldn't shoot at anyone sporting a red cross.

The Marines eventually seized Bouresches and by June 26, 1918, had gained control of all of Belleau Wood — a feat that the French Army had been unable to do for four years. The victory effectively prevented the Germans from reaching the French capital of Paris. But it came at a high price. The Americans suffered nearly 4,600 casualties.

Three weeks later, the 49th Company was tasked with helping the French retake the town of Soissons. Nice and his men had gone three nights without sleep and hadn't had any food for two days, because they had been on the move and supplies hadn't caught up with them. Nevertheless, the leathernecks were ready to fight.

On July 18, the Marines charged the Germans, who greeted them with a five-minute barrage that felled hundreds of Americans. *It's like all the guns in the world have opened up on us,* Nice thought as he raced from one shell hole to another. Despite the strong stand by the enemy, the Marines gained ground over the next couple of days.

On the third night of the battle, Nice led a patrol of fifty-six men on a mission to locate a German battalion that had retreated. Going deep into enemy territory, Nice and his comrades found the Germans — and the Germans found the Marines. Cut off from friendly forces, the American patrol was surrounded. But not for long.

Probing for any weakness in the enemy cordon, Nice directed his men in a pitched battle, hoping to break free. Suddenly, an enemy bullet ripped through his right forearm, causing him to drop his rifle. He picked up his weapon and kept on shooting. Eventually, the patrol fought its way back to its battalion. Only nineteen of his men returned unscathed — the rest were wounded or killed.

Because he sustained only a flesh wound, Nice refused to go to the first-aid station and instead used a bandage to wrap the bullet hole in his arm.

"Gunner," said a fellow leatherneck, "you're one tough son of a gun."

Nice grinned and, using a new term for the Marines that was gaining popularity, replied, "Just call me a Devil Dog."

By the fourth and final day of the Battle of Soissons, the Allied offensive had advanced six miles and captured around three thousand prisoners, eleven artillery batteries, and one hundred machine guns — some of which were turned on the retreating enemy.

In September, at the Battle of St. Mihiel, Nice and his comrades slogged through knee-deep mud and driving rain in a difficult offensive against the Germans. One particular enemy machine gun nest was causing the 49th Company the most trouble, so Nice took four men and set out to silence it for good. They crawled through muck and water. They were so completely covered in mud that they were perfectly camouflaged, which allowed them to sneak up on the enemy machine gunners.

"On the count of three, throw your grenades," he whispered to his men. "One . . . two . . . three!" Rising to their knees, they hurled their grenades in unison, all landing directly into the nest, killing the eight-man enemy unit.

The four-day battle was another success for the Americans, but the division had suffered tremendous losses of veteran soldiers — many of them close friends of Nice's who had fought by his side in other lands.

In October, the Marines joined Allied forces in a pivotal battle near the town of St. Etienne at Blanc Mont, a ridgeline of white limestone that the Germans had turned into an impenetrable fortress. On the bluff overlooking the killing field below, the enemy had placed Maxims about ten yards apart. For four years, Blanc Mont had been shelled, machine gunned, bombed, and assaulted by the French and then the British, but to no avail. Any infantry unit that dared to attack it was cut to ribbons by the deeply entrenched Maxims and artillery.

The mission to take Blanc Mont ridge was given to the experienced doughboys and Marines of the AEF's Second Division, which included Nice's 49th Company.

Before the initial assault, his pal, Lieutenant Connor, confided to him, "I guess I'm getting yellow. If the old man [Captain Hamilton] sent me to the rear now, I'd go."

"Yellow?" snorted Nice. "There isn't a better nor a braver soldier in the whole AEF or any other army than you."

"Well," persisted Connor, "I've got a hunch I'm not coming back from this battle."

Nice waved off the comment and told Connor, "Oh, snap out of it. You're just talking this way because we haven't eaten in a couple of days. All that's wrong with you is an empty belly."

Seconds before going over the top at 5:50 A.M. on a gray, misty October 3, 1918, Nice, the other platoon leaders, and front-line sergeants made eye contact with one another to make sure everyone was focused. *We're ready,* he thought.

Out in front of the assault force, French and American artillery opened with earthshaking crashes of shellfire bursting in red-and-green flames in orderly rows on the enemy lines. Black clouds of smoke billowed up where larger shells exploded on the hillside.

With no cover and totally exposed to the enemy above them, the Marines took hundreds upon hundreds of casualties during the first hour. Nice tried to ignore the carnage and kept urging his men forward.

Lieutenant Connor, leader of the first platoon, was about forty paces away from Nice, who was in charge of the second platoon. As the two platoons reached the bottom edge of the slope, the ground shook from enemy artillery rounds. One of the shells exploded right next to Connor, launching him in the air.

"Chuck! Chuck!" shouted Nice, running over to his friend. Connor was sprawled on the ground, his broken, bleeding body sliced from head to toe with shrapnel. Nice carried a small first-aid kit and quickly pulled out a bandage, but it was no use. He knew it and Connor knew it.

Unable to talk, Connor smiled, patted Nice on the arm, and died.

Nice bowed his head and said, "You were a prince of a man."

A nearby bomb dropped by one of the dozens of German airplanes circling overhead showered Nice with dirt and debris. *The best thing I can do for Chuck is to kill as many* Boches *as possible,* he thought.

By noon, the battle had intensified. Just when Nice thought it couldn't get any worse, it did. The Germans used gas, forcing the leathernecks to don masks in the worst gas attack that Nice had ever experienced. With masks on, artillery shells bursting all around them, and machine guns firing from the front, left, and right, the soldiers were easy targets.

Through it all, Nice moved his men — those who weren't badly wounded or dead — to a wooded spot on the slope that provided some cover. Then he jumped into a shell hole where he found Hamilton firing his rifle.

"I've organized the company sector with twenty men, Captain," Nice reported. "They're all we got left. You and I make twenty-two. Lord, I'm tired. What I don't understand is why we're still alive."

"We're lucky," said Hamilton. "Lucky and good."

The few Marines left in the company pressed on. Some actually made it beyond their objective and ended up enduring withering flanking fire before they retreated in confusion.

After finally reaching the top of Blanc Mont, Captain Hamilton told Nice, "We have reports of stragglers still wandering around out there lost and not sure where they should go. We need a patrol to round them up."

"I'll gather some men and pick up the lost soldiers," Nice volunteered. While heading back into the killing zone, Nice was struck in the thigh with a machine gun bullet that left him writhing on the ground. With the help of his comrades, he limped back to his company.

Seeing how badly he was wounded, Hamilton ordered, "You need to go to the rear for treatment."

"But, Captain," Nice protested. "I don't want to leave my men. I feel well enough to stay and fight. The wound isn't that bad."

"I can tell it's worse," Hamilton said. "I'm ordering you to the rear. If you don't go, you face a court martial. Now get out of here!"

Reluctantly, Nice let the medics take him to the hospital near Paris. The next night in the ward, he met an officer, Captain Kelly, from another Marine unit. The two talked about how much they wanted to return to their outfits.

"Forget about waiting days before we get a hospital discharge," said Kelly. "Let's leave now and get back to the fight."

"That's a grand idea," said Nice.

They slipped out of the hospital and hitchhiked to Paris, hoping to find transportation back to the front, even though neither had any money. But then they were stopped by the military police. When the two Marines couldn't produce any traveling orders that gave them permission to be in Paris, they were taken to the brig and charged with being AWOL.

Fortunately, the officer who was in charge of the provost guard was sympathetic to their plight. "You boys don't deserve to be locked up, especially since you've both been wounded and still want to return to the front," said the officer. "Here." He handed them passes and tickets on a train that would take them closer to their units. When he learned they had no money, he gave them twenty francs so they could get something to eat.

"There's no need to pay me back," he said. "Just win the war."

"Oh, we will, sir," replied Nice. "We most definitely will."

Nice received eleven medals and citations — including the Croix de Guerre and the Silver Star — for his heroic efforts during the war.

Fully recovered from his wounds, he returned to America after the war and settled in Manasquan, New Jersey, where he got married, raised a family, and made a career in the financial field. The bullet that wounded him in the back remained in him the rest of his life.

WWI GLOSSARY

ace fighter pilot who has shot down at least five enemy planes

AEF abbreviation for the American Expeditionary Forces, the name given the United States military forces active in Europe during the war

aerodrome European term for small airfield

Allies the alliance of nations, mainly France, the British Empire (including Canada), Russia, Romania, Serbia, and later joined by the United States, Japan, and Italy, who all fought against the Central Powers

Armistice the official agreement between the Allies and Germany that caused a cease-fire on November 11, 1918

AWOL abbreviation for Absent Without Leave

barrage artillery bombardment

battalion a military unit of 300 to 1,200 troops from two to seven companies

battery an artillery unit of large guns, cannons, and mortars

bayonet a blade attached to the end of a rifle for close-quarter fighting

Boche insulting nickname for German soldiers

brancardier French term for stretcher bearers

brig Navy jail

Central Powers an alliance between Germany, Austria-Hungary, Turkey, and Bulgaria

cordon line of soldiers surrounding an enemy area to control access

Croix de Guerre French military medal awarded for valor during combat

depth bomb or **depth charge** a waterproof bomb that only detonates at a certain depth to attack submarines

Devil Dogs nickname for Marines

Distinguished Service Cross the second-highest American military award for extreme gallantry during combat

dogfight aerial battle

doughboy popular nickname for an American soldier

dugout a shelter dug out of the side of a trench, varying from a small hole to a large underground room

Eastern Front the area of conflict between Russia, Germany, and Austria-Hungary located to the east of Germany and Austria-Hungary

flank the left or right side of a military unit's position

flanking fire shooting at the side of a military unit's position

Flying Circus Allied nickname for the German squadron of elite pilots led by Manfred von Richthofen, better known as the infamous Red Baron

funk hole a small hole dug by a soldier for protection. Called "fox holes" in later wars.

Hindenburg Line a connected series of German defensive fortifications on the Western Front

Kamerad German term for "pal" or "comrade," used by German troops to surrender

Luger a German semiautomatic pistol

No Man's Land the dangerous ground between opposing lines of trenches

over the top climbing up and out of a trench to attack the enemy

poste de secours French term for first-aid station

regiment military unit consisting of three to five battalions

shrapnel fragments, such as steel balls and metal shards, that are scattered when an artillery shell, grenade, or bomb explodes

sortie mission flown by a combat aircraft

tracer glowing ammunition used to aid aiming

trench mortar a short cannon that launches shells designed to drop on enemy trenches

victory the shooting down by an Allied pilot of an enemy plane or balloon

water jacket a water-filled compartment that cools a machine gun

Western Front the battle line between the Allies and the Germans extending from the Swiss border along the western border of Germany and into northeastern France to the North Sea

ABOUT THE AUTHOR

Allan Zullo is the author of more than one hundred nonfiction books on subjects ranging from sports and the supernatural to history and animals.

He has introduced Scholastic readers to the Ten True Tales series, gripping stories of extraordinary persons who have met the challenges of dangerous, sometimes life-threatening, situations. Among the books in the series are *FBI Heroes*; *Heroes of 9/11*; *World War II Heroes*; *War Heroes: Voices from Iraq*; *Battle Heroes: Voices from Afghanistan*; and *Combat Heroes: Voices from Vietnam*.

In addition, he has authored four books about the real-life experiences of young people during the Holocaust: *Survivors: True Stories of Children in the Holocaust*; *Heroes of the Holocaust: True Stories of Rescues by Teens*; *Escape: Children of the Holocaust*; and *We Fought Back: Teen Resisters of the Holocaust*.

Allan, the father of two grown daughters and the grand-father of five, lives with his wife, Kathryn, near Asheville, North Carolina. To learn more about the author, visit his Website at www.allanzullo.com.